Riding the Wave: Lessons in
Leadership from my 43-Year Career
at the Walt Disney Company

ENGAGE, INSPIRE, LEAD

JIM MACPHEE

No part of this publication may be reproduced, stored in a retrieval system, or transmitted in any form or by any means, electronic, mechanical, photocopying, recording, or otherwise, without written permission of the author. For information regarding permission, please contact the author.

ISBN: 978-1-956464-15-3

All rights reserved.
Published in the United States of America by BrightRay Publishing.

This book is intended to provide commentary on life and leadership based on the author's experiences. While their previous employer is cited, this book was not written with their endorsement, collaboration, or any other involvement. The views and opinions expressed within this book are the author's alone and do not necessarily reflect that of their previous employer's. No copyrighted material or proprietary information is deliberately shared within this book, and any unintended usage of such should be considered as "Fair Use" for educational purposes and commentary made by the author (Section 107, US Copyright Law). This book is based on the recollection of the author's and the author's alone, and so the information is not guaranteed to be wholly accurate (dates, times, locations, etcetera). The author and publisher does not assume any liability for any usage or application of the information within.

TABLE OF CONTENTS

Dedication, vii

Testimonies from Colleagues, ix

Introduction, xxiii

BACKGROUND

    Pre-Disney 2

    Decade I 12

    Decade II 29

    Decade III 44

    The Next Generation Experience 57

    Decade IV 70

INTRODUCTION TO INSPIRATIONAL LEADERSHIP

ENGAGE

    Introduction: Relationships Matter! 108

    RIKC 115

    DiversiFY Everything! 125

    Humility and Vulnerability 128

    Trust 134

    Look Outside Yourself 141

    Be Bold, Be Brave 148

    Summary 152

INSPIRE

Introduction: Transform Hearts and Minds 154

Make Work Fun 158

Connect to Your Purpose 164

Storytelling 169

Commitment 179

Summary 184

LEAD

Introduction 186

Clarity, Unity, and Agility 191

Strengthen Your Core 195

Lead with a Holistic Mindset 198

Leading with a Transformative Mindset 209

Heritage and Tradition 219

Integrity 223

Balance Art and Science 230

Presence 234

Feed the Good Wolf 240

Summary 243

Conclusion, 245

Sources, 249

Acknowledgements, 253

About the Author, 271

DEDICATION

This book is dedicated to my family.

To Mom and Dad...thank you for your love, kindness, support, adventures and the oh-so-many life lesson you imparted upon me. You taught me the wisdom of the importance to dream, to be authentic, and to live life to its fullest. I wish you were on this planet to see us in action, but I know you are watching and guiding us from above.

To my brothers and sister...Kathy, Dan and Scott...thank you for an incredible life well lived and for always being there for me, my family and for each other. Thank you for the wonderful adventures, memories, laughs and love throughout our journey together!

To my nieces and nephews...Andrew, Sarah, Michael, Laurel, Addison, Michael and Colin...thank you for the energy and spirit you carry in this world...the MacPhee legacy is in your hands...carry it well! May you live your best life and change the world!

To Marty, Anna, Carter, ^JJ^ and Cabo...thank you for your love, laughter, inspiration and spirit. You've taught me what's most important in life, you've supported me through really great times and really rough ones. You are my purpose for living. I am so incredibly grateful for your unconditional love and support. I love you truly, madly, deeply.

TESTIMONIES FROM COLLEAGUES

It is uncharacteristic of me to share personal notes of appreciation, but I wanted to include a selection I received from my dear colleagues and friends upon my retirement. I thank each and every one of you for the kind words, and I hope you all know that I will treasure these forever.

> Jim said, GET IN THE PARK, WALK ALONGSIDE THE TEAM
> SAY HELLO TO THE CAST THAT ARE SOMETIMES UNSEEN
> HE MADE US THINK WHEN WE THOUGHT THAT WE KNEW
> HE MADE US LAUGH WITH THE THINGS THAT HE'D DO
> HE MADE US HUMAN WHEN WE GOT LOST IN THE RULES
> HE MADE US BALANCE WHEN WE GOT STUCK IN ONE VIEW
> HE SAID, FEED THE GOOD WOLF, WHEN HE SENSED WE WERE OFF
> HE COULD LIFT UP OUR SPIRITS WHEN WE WERE JUST ABOUT LOST
> HE COULD RALLY THE TROOPS WITH JUST A FEW NOTES
> NO PODIUM, NO SCRIPT — JUST CLEAR VISION ... AND HOPE
> HE SAID, LEADERSHIP MATTERS ... IT SOUNDS LIKE OLD NEWS
> BUT HE DIDN'T JUST SAY IT, HE WALKED IN THOSE SHOES
> JIM MADE US ALL BETTER ... HIS IMPRINT IS CLEAR
> AND NOW HE'S GONE FROM HIS OFFICE ... BUT HE'LL ALWAYS BE HERE

Wow. What a day. I must admit, I feel a bit sad and empty when I think about you heading out. But, what else would I expect when someone that has been such a force...for so many...and particularly for me...sets off for his next chapter? You have changed who I am and who I want to be. No exaggeration. Going to miss you.

But so, so happy for you and your family. Cherish the day…and celebrate what you have done for so many.

Josh D'Amaro, Chairman of Parks, Experiences and Products

◇◇◇◇◇◇◇◇◇◇◇◇◇◇◇◇◇◇◇◇

I can not imagine anyone more qualified to write a book entitled Engage, Inspire, and Lead! I had the privilege of watching Jim do all of those for many years. He is a gifted leader and an extraordinary human being. So many want the answer to the question "How does Disney do it?". My answer is that the "magic" is the result of a very special brand of leadership…the kind of leadership that Jim role modeled every day of his career.

Meg Crofton, former President of Walt Disney Parks & Resorts Operations, U.S. and France

◇◇◇◇◇◇◇◇◇◇◇◇◇◇◇◇◇◇◇◇

You and I discussed a number of times how the true magic of Disney Parks is generated, protected, and sustained by the cast members who work there. It's amazing and inspiring to think about how long you have been a part of that magic. As you reinforced consistently through both words and actions, each of the thousands and thousands of cast members is important to fulfilling the promise of Disney magic.

Nonetheless, there are a few—but not many—cast members, current or past, who have truly shaped the magic and been a constant source of energy and inspiration for all those around them. You, my friend, are clearly one of those few.

It was a joy and a privilege for me to call you a colleague during my time at Disney. I looked forward to every walk-through, meeting, or event with you. No matter the topic or situation, you would approach it positively and optimistically and look for an opportunity to contribute. I know that you had exactly the same effect on every person who had the pleasure to work with you.

Patti Smith once said that your legacy is how many hearts you've touched. Your legacy is enormous, positive and profound. It lives in the millions of guests who have enjoyed what you made possible for them at the parks, the cast members you inspired, trained, and mentored, and the friends whose lives you enriched throughout. I'm pleased and thankful to have been in all three of those categories!

Tom Staggs, former Chief Operating Officer for the Walt Disney Company

It is rare to find qualities of leadership that shine so clearly, but Jim's open and authentic style at Walt Disney World in everything he did and said, made him an incredible mentor to those he led, and an inspirational role model to those who aspired to lead. If just a fraction of that magic is passed on in this book, it will be an essential guiding-light for those on their own path to lead. I can't think of a better companion than Jim.

Catherine Powell, former President of Disney Parks, Western Region

---

There are so many things for you to feel proud of with your career. I consider myself quite fortunate for our working time together. You always made things fun! I know that during the last several years it has been tough as nails, but you can consider yourself the winner in all of it!

Erin Wallace, former EVP of Walt Disney Parks & Resorts, Operations

Jim is a dedicated husband and father, a beacon for what is great in our heritage and a courageous friend.

Jim has taken on so many exciting opportunities in his career, and he has always boldly embraced new assignments. Starting in 1978 as a watercraft pilot, he has had multiple assignments throughout our business that included Disney's Hollywood Studios, Disney's Animal Kingdom, Disneyland, Line of Business Attractions, Epcot, NGE, and finally leading all of our Parks at Walt Disney World. Jim made each area better by having been there. More importantly, Jim developed great leaders and meaningful friendships along the way.

Jim let me know of his plans to retire in our first meeting in May after I took on my current role. Since then, Jim has never slowed down. He has continued with the same passion and energy to help lead us through these difficult times. Without him, we would not be where we are today in our path forward.

Jeff Vahle, President of Walt Disney World Resort

Great Executive Leadership teams are often defined by the combination of unique qualities and talents that reside among the team. Jim MacPhee has been the glue that has helped bring together

Executive teams in both Florida and California. His unique style of humor balanced with the truth, deep subject matter expertise and an uncanny ability to make work really fun helped to define the Disney Parks culture and in doing so helped our thousands of Cast Members create millions of Magical Memories for our Guests. Jim MacPhee is the total Executive package - "just push play"!!

George Kalogridis, President of Segment Development and Enrichment for Disney Parks, Experiences and Products

---

Quote that reminds me of Jim:

"Which wolf wins?" – "The one you feed"

Funny Story about Jim:

"I constantly lectured him on eating different food and he sincerely enjoyed breaking this rule in front of me with remarkable consistency."

What I learned from Jim:

"Speak up with immense conviction and passion when you believe in something."

What I admire most about Jim:

"Courage combined with integrity is the foundation of Jim."

Reflection of Jim's Leadership legacy:

"Leadership matters, Culture matters, People matter."

My wishes to Jim as he embarks on his next chapter:

"Jim, the most important thing in life is knowing the most important things in life."

Thomas Mazloum, President of Disney Signature Experiences

We have been on quite the journey together; I feel so blessed to have you in my life! I'll never forget our first project; opening up Disney MGM studios with the PowWow Event where it was POURING rain. But it was the start of something wonderful. We would always arm wrestle to this day on what park events we should or shouldn't do. Then we had a great time in CA together and got to work through some crazy times! But the highlight for me was returning to WDW in 2015 and getting to work side by side with you. Learning and watching you in action was so impressive. Your hashtag #leadership matters, is truly an example of "walking the talk." Thanks for being feedback rich, supporting me professionally and personally and just being an awesome friend! This isn't goodbye as I know we will keep in touch and catch up regularly! Love you my friend.

Claire Bilby, SVP, Signature Experience Services

Everything I needed to know about Leadership I learned from Jim MacPhee...

- God, Faith and Family should always remain first.
- You can crush any force against you with determination, best in class doctors & the right mindset.
- Mentors are built through trust, vulnerability and conversations.
- Leadership really does matter.
- Relationships are key to making things happen.
- Ride the Ride Path—go ahead of others to ensure all goes well.
- Caring for others always comes first.
- Great leaders have humility balanced with courage.
- You may not have the title, but you can act the part.
- Engage others and make them feel important, ask for their opinion.
- Celebrating work accomplishments is expected but showing up for personal milestones is what makes the difference (my wedding, birth of my twins).

- Communication is key for change management to occur.
- You can be a spotlight holder and have just as much pride.
- Have Fun—we should laugh often.
- Know others likes / dislikes—corn, oh well we missed that one!
- Protein will sustain us—order the nuts and cheese for the snack.
- Friends become the family we choose.
- Collaboration is key to our collective success.
- Informal can be as powerful as formal.
- Respect others opinions even if you disagree.
- Sharing your story inspires others.
- Credibility is earned through relationships, knowledge and influence (RIKC).
- Inspirational leadership is a gift to others.

Jim, your constant encouragement, and belief in me has truly changed my life. You celebrated life with me at work and personal (wedding, twins, etc). I am beyond grateful to God for blessing me with such an amazing leader and dear friend that I consider family. I will be proudly carrying your torch and teaching all you taught me to others – this is how your legacy will live on...

Deb Hart, Vice President of Operations at Walt Disney World

Jambo Jimbo!

I remember vividly the first time we talked in person which was me interviewing for a job at Disney's Animal Kingdom. It was clear to me in that interaction that you were someone who viewed the world in an optimistic and forward looking way. I would come to know later how much you would shape the way that I approached the work.

You have a special way to make people feel comfortable around you while still demanding excellence. You took key moments of failure at times and made them catch phrases like "ride the ride path" which was a direct reference to being caught in an unexpected circumstance because the proper preparation was not done. You used this phrase routinely to make sure your direct reports understood what was expected, but also what you expected of yourself in the process.

The most important thing that I appreciated is your warm and caring engagement with seemingly all that you encountered. Most people that I interacted with had a story about how you either reached them on a personal or professional level. You have a deeper way to connect and inspire people and have been someone I have admired and appreciated in a way that is more profound than you probably realize.

In the end we are measured by the way we have impacted that people that will carry on with the business of making magic. You should be very proud of the way you have shaped the culture and people that you have come in contact with. I will forever be grateful for the time we spent together and the advice that you gave to me. I will miss having you in the workplace but I hope to be back in the area sometime in the future so we can connect in person.

*Joe Schott, President and GM
at Shanghai Disney Resort*

It is hard to believe that this day has actually come. Though I have known it was coming, it was something I kept denying.

To say I will miss you day in and day out is the understatement of the year.

It is really hard to put into words what our friendship has meant to me so I will call upon a few people who articulated it better than I.

Steve Marboli once wrote: "Friends are medicine for a wounded heart, and vitamins for a hopeful soul."

There were many years there that you and I both thought we were going to go over the cliff. I would say that YOU are the primary reason I survived that time. I remained hopeful for a brighter future and you always made me believe in our purpose. It made me want to be better and do better. You were good medicine.

Absolutely no one can make me laugh as you can, and it has helped me get through hard times and great times, and will be one of my greatest memories of you. Me laughing and ALWAYS getting caught while you looked innocently away.

Thank you from the bottom of my heart for what you taught me, for how you supported me, and for always being a beacon of truth and light.

I will end by sharing one of my favorite quotes by Eleanor Roosevelt that so clearly captures my feelings:

Many people will walk in and out of your life, but only true friends will have footprints in your heart.

You will forever have a footprint in my heart.

Maribeth Bisienere, SVP of Resorts, Transportation, Premium Services, and Food & Beverage at the Walt Disney Company

◇◇◇◇◇◇◇◇◇◇◇◇◇◇◇◇◇◇◇◇◇◇

I miss you already! There was an immediate, spiritual connection during our first conversation, and you have been like family ever since. Thank you for welcoming me with open arms, for helping me find my footing and for always, always being there for me whether I needed a well-timed distraction (your GIF game is STRONG!) or your experienced perspective.

Leadership DOES matter and I appreciate yours. I love you, friend.

Roz Durant, SVP of Operations at Walt Disney World

---

ex·pe·ri·ence

/ˌikˈspirēəns/: the way you always made me feel...Smart. Valued. Respected. Included. Funny. Loved. Talented. Trustworthy. Influential. Knowledgeable. Credible. #RIKCmatters!

trans·for·ma·tion

\/ˌtran(t)sfərˈmāSH(ə)n/ : how you changed my life... gave me a seat at the table and pulled me into Ops, trusted me despite being "green", grew my mind and heart in ways I never could have imagined, taught me that bravery is more important than perfection, demonstrated that everyone matters regardless of rank, title, seniority, experience, knowledge, or position, showed me that laughter and perseverance is the life blood of challenges, and let me have a life with my family and my children. But most of all, allowed me - and celebrated me - for being myself. For honoring my desire to be a mom first. For never letting me fall to my ego. For letting my values in life guide me and always, always helping me stay true to them. You truly built

TESTIMONIES FROM COLLEAGUES

my strengths and gave me confidence in my true, authentic self, and gave me confidence that I never had before.

They say that in life, there are those people that are truly heaven sent. That God placed there for a reason. And I count you among my most special blessings in my entire life.

Do what you love.
Love what you do.
Love who you do it with!

I love you and thank you for everything you have given me. And so does my family!!

"What we do in life echoes in eternity" and so does your legacy, it forever lives on in all of the lives you touched in so many ways.

Wishing you all the love and laughter this life has to offer and so much more in your next chapter!

Xoxo

Natalie Sirianni, Experience Manager, Operations at Walt Disney World

INTRODUCTION

If you had told me when I'd just been hired that I would spend the next four-plus decades with the most powerful entertainment company in the world, I'm not sure how I would have responded. If you had told me halfway through my career that I would be directly involved with radical innovation of the vacation experience, that would have blown my mind. And if you had told me a year ago that I would be an author, I don't know if I'd even believe it. Then again, I never could have anticipated most of what I've gotten to do. My life has been a series of unexpected, but often amazing, experiences.

I was blessed with a nearly 43-year career at Disney. I started by driving watercraft vessels on Bay Lake and the Seven Seas Lagoon in 1978 before traveling across the Walt Disney World landscape and a couple of years in California, and ended my career leading teams across all of Operations as the Senior Vice President of Operations for the Walt Disney World Resort. Externally, this is known as the Chief Operating Officer or COO. Beyond the title, I got to be a part of enabling extraordinary experiences for our cast members and our guests, and worked with so many incredible people along the way. That's all that really mattered.

The ride's been fun, but it hasn't been without pain and hardship. My incredible wife Marty gave birth to our triplets, Anna, Carter, and James IV (JJ), prematurely at only 26 weeks and tragically, JJ passed away when he was only three weeks old. My parents both passed away much too early from cancer before I received my own diagnosis, a journey I've been on since the last decade of my career. I intimately understand the fragility of life, and my perspective has been forever changed as a result.

I might be retired now, but this isn't going to be a history lesson or some big reflection on the past. Looking in the rearview mirror for too long can distract you from the path ahead...I've learned that the hard way! But as I've thought about the past and everything I've learned from it, one thing is clear—life is fleeting. Our time on this planet is finite and therefore, the relationships we can build with others is the purpose we have to fulfill while we're here, along with the legacy we leave.

I have been privileged to have worked with so many people and do a variety of things throughout my career at Disney. And as it turns out, the lessons I've learned have been far beyond academics. It's been those cherished moments I've experienced—the good, the bad, and the ugly. They've all shaped who I am and how I go about the world...I call this my "PhD in life."

This is only to say that what you have on your CV doesn't define you. Your title and achievements aren't really your legacy, either. At the end of my career, I was surprised and touched to have been given permanent presence in the Magic Kingdom via a window on Main Street, U.S.A. To have your name painted on the windows overlooking the park's entrance is an incredible honor that only a few have received. I am so grateful to be one of them.

And while this window, which I share with three very special colleagues, will forever be a wonderful memory and honor, this piece of glass is only a tangible representation of my legacy. My legacy won't really be just the material objects—it'll be the relationships that I've built with people I'll cherish for the rest of my life. That's my wife, my children, my coworkers, my friends, and everyone else I've ever interacted with. I can only hope that I've given them even an ounce of what they've all given me.

I'm not looking to write a historical play-by-play of Walt Disney World over the last four decades. And I don't want this to be an academic work on C-suite corporate tactics, either. This book begins with an overview of the incredible career I've had and then segues into a collection of the principles and beliefs I've developed through a series of experience that have shaped me to become a better human all around—a better husband, father, brother, friend, and yes, a better leader as well. As a side note, I despise repetitive use of "I," so please forgive me for doing so myself. This introduction is definitely littered with them! However, it is necessary to share about myself and my story in order to share what I have gained from it.

I was privileged to spend many years leading tens of thousands of people to create the magic for millions and millions of guests at Walt Disney World. Now, I feel a responsibility to share the many lessons I have learned throughout my career. That is ultimately what this book is about. Actually, that is what leadership is about.

These 301 pages come down to the four principles on the cover: engage, inspire, lead...*relationships matter!* Sounds simple, right? It's not.

While I did recognize the impact great leaders had early in my career, I eventually came to understand the full meaning of and actions behind these words, and how incredibly impactful they can be to individuals and organizations. In addition, it became clear that *leadership matters*, and I spent my last few years really focusing on illuminating the importance of that statement.

Since retiring, I've reflected on this dynamic and have come to realize that *relationships matter* even more, as building relationships serves as the catalyst for inspiring people to go above and beyond...further than they ever even realized.

I've come to realize that, yes, leadership matters—at work. But relationships define both your personal life and individual leadership more than anyone would imagine. Life is made up of our relationships with others, and that carries into the workplace. You won't be able to get the best out of people unless you build commitment with them by connecting on an authentic level first.

Right now, the world at large is contending with a serious lack of inspiration and engagement, especially in the workplace. Many people often don't know their organization's why, don't understand how they contribute toward it, and many don't feel that they are on a team. Their jobs have often become 8-hour acts that don't build into any greater purpose. And it's not really their fault—even our best leaders find it challenging to lead and motivate across a multigenerational workforce. How one person can be engaged and inspired can look very different from how another person is, and many leaders haven't figured out how to make that distinction. This has never been more true than it is today, because the new generations entering the workforce are looking for a connection, a purpose, a Why, more than ever.

Some leadership books will tell you how to classify everyone as a certain personality type and what tactics will work best "on" them. But the truth is that each person you encounter is a unique individual too complex to neatly fit within some category. There's no definitive formula to inspirational leadership.

The solution, however, is just as simple. All you have to do is *develop relationships* with those around you to engage, inspire, and lead them to success. Being authentic and, as a result, even vulnerable, in the workplace is not easy, but it is ultimately the only answer.

So, yes, leadership matters, but the energy and enthusiasm we instill in one another—agnostic of what our business cards, titles, or roles imply—matters most. How and why we engage and inspire is what creates our legacy. My hope is that by sharing what I've learned, I can ignite your own leadership—and your relationships—and inspire you to make an impact to infinity and beyond.

To start, I'll take it back to the beginning. I was born on a cloudy day...

Just kidding. But if you're willing to hang with me for the first half or so of this book as I tell you the experiences that shaped my philosophy, I'll tell you the principles and beliefs that I've lived by to be an effective leader.

BACKGROUND

Pre-Disney

This is going to sound like such a cliche, but it's just the truth—my early years were the foundation of who I am today. While nobody's background can necessarily define them, how we grow up will come to shape who we are and who we have become. Our childhoods are formative in hindsight, too. We don't grow up fully aware that we're "growing up." We just enjoy life in the moment, in whatever circumstances that may be.

In the back row: Dad, Mom, me, and Kathy. In the front row: Dan and Scott.

I was very fortunate to have been raised the way I was—two great parents, three siblings, almost always outdoors. We were fortunate to have grown up close to both the Atlantic Ocean and the Halifax River on the Intercoastal Waterway in Ormond Beach, Florida.

My dad, also named Jim, worked very hard to become a dentist and establish his own practice in Ormond Beach, Florida. He was a self-made and successful man. After serving in the Navy, he put himself through dental school with the support of Mom…while raising twins at the same time! I don't mean that he was "successful" in the sense of pure income, though. He counted his riches not in money, but in the fulfillment of his dreams. I fondly remember the wisdom he imparted on all of us in his latter stage of life: "Keep on dreaming." Dad was all about living life to its fullest—you can probably tell where I got the whole *carpe diem* thing from, right?

Linda, my mom, had quite a few titles. Aside from the unquestionable family matriarch and a devout Episcopalian, she was also CEO (Chief Experience Officer) and CUD (Chief Uber Driver). She ran much of our family operations, including schlepping all of us to a myriad of activities and extracurriculars. She was also very active in her church, fulfilling her faith, and was one heck of a chef too. Mom taught us so much about so many subjects, and we gained so much wisdom from her.

I've got a twin sister and two brothers. Kathy is technically the oldest by a couple minutes, and Dan and Scott are younger by a couple years. From very early on, my parents instilled in us the importance of pursuing our dreams. They wanted us to go out and find what we wanted to do, whatever that was. This was the wisdom that especially my dad, until his last breath on this planet, worked to impart on his children and grandchildren. He lived his life as an example for all of us, and his example showed that life was about doing something you like and enjoying everything outside of work, too.

My parents practiced what they preached, and they did a lot to provide us with amazing experiences and opportunities to see the world. Even as young children, we traveled in a motorhome from down to the Keys all the way up to the mountains of North Carolina. They were very much the outdoorsy kind of people, and they took us on their many adventures.

Being so close to the water was a big part of our life. We first lived just a few blocks from the Atlantic Ocean and then eventually moved "across the river" to the mainland, where we came to enjoy the intercoastal waterways just as much. In the eighteen years that I was a resident within the family household, we all came together for more than a few of what I call "adventure chapters"—family phases of scuba diving, sailing, camping, fishing, and other activities.

Family time in the Bahamas aboard Dad's boat, Vesla III. That's me on the windsurfer.

My dad was a part of the Ormond Beach Anchor Chasers Diver Club. All six of us got our scuba diving certifications and went reef and wreck diving in the Bahamas several times a year. More often, we'd go down to the beach and have barbeques, bonfires, and camp out. After we moved to the mainland, my dad also got a family sailboat to take everyone out for offshore fun. Between being on land or water, wherever we landed, my parents made sure we understood and appreciated the natural world around us.

Each of us eventually settled into our own particular thing. Dan was the consummate fisherman and spent time on the beach as a lifeguard. Scott was a lifeguard too, but he really thrived on the high school soccer team. Kathy was into cheerleading and worked in the hospitality field around Daytona.

My thing was surfing. I started out pretty young, about 13 years old. Since we were just a few blocks away from the ocean, it was so easy for me to grab my board and head to the beach. After we moved inland, I'd either have to take my surfboard on a jon boat and row across the river or strap it to my bike and ride over the Granada Bridge. I'm sure that was quite a sight to any passing cars, especially when the wind was howling, but the extra distance didn't matter to me—I wanted to hit the waves.

As fun as it is, surfing definitely isn't easy. Nature is beautiful, but shifting. You never know what you're going to get. It could be gliding on glass-like waters, or it could be riding massive swells across the sea. And sometimes, you're not going to get anything at all. Sometimes, you have to just hang out there and wait for whatever is to come. The ability to roll with whatever and be patient doesn't come naturally to a lot of people, especially to teenage boys. I had to develop some serious sea legs to weather through rough and smooth seas alike.

I truly believe in the zen of the ocean. The water is constantly and completely shifting. Out there, what happened a minute ago is already past and what will happen a minute from now cannot be predicted. It's all about *this* moment, and no other one. When you're on the water, you come to fully appreciate what's happening right now. There's not much else like it.

In these early years outdoors, I learned to read the environment and understand the elements within it. I knew the whims of nature were out of my control. There was no changing the will of the world around me. I developed the ability to accept the conditions as they are and navigate accordingly. Looking back, that has come to be immensely helpful throughout my life.

My parents encouraged us to go out and experience all the different adventures of life. That meant the adventures of work, too. I understood the importance of getting a job pretty young. If I wanted spending money, I'd have to earn it. My parents supported my employment pursuits for teenage income early on.

My first venture into the working world was as a paperboy. I was about 12 when I signed up to deliver *The Halifax News Journal* in the neighborhood. I was an active kid with a Schwinn bike perfectly designed for the big bag of newspapers to be positioned right between the handlebars for me to easily access for "the toss." It seemed like all the stars were aligned for me to be the best-in-class paperboy.

Turns out, I had *no* idea what I'd really signed up for! Before our digital age of instant information, the morning paper was essential. I, a barely teenaged kid, now had this massive responsibility to ensure that a vast number of households would get the news. It was a big burden for someone who thought they'd just be casually riding around like they did in the movies.

The papers came in giant stacks around 2 in the morning. They didn't come ready-to-go, by the way. I had to wake up at 4 am to sort, fold, and bundle them myself, then load them up and start the route by 5, aboard my Schwinn bicycle. For a first job, that was a lot, but I understood the importance of my role and carried that pretty heavily.

Honestly, I don't think I did a great job. Really honestly, it was kind of a disaster. I would say I overslept about 50% of the time. Thank God for Mom, who I'd have to wake up to drive me through my route, or else the paper wouldn't be delivered on time.

Safe to say this was a pretty short-lived venture. However, I wasn't deterred from other jobs. From that whole paper route debacle, I realized two things. One, I am most definitely not a morning person. And two, I probably shouldn't be left to my own devices like that, at least at that age. I needed a little bit more structure and discipline, which most other jobs provided. So I decided to move on.

My very first clock-in job was as a busser at the Village Inn Pancake House, often working with my buddy Steve. I'd bike to work in my full uniform (I had to wear a bow tie, but that stayed in my pocket until absolutely necessary) usually with my surfboard strapped to the back, work 7 am to maybe 2 pm, change into my baggies, and then surf the rest of the afternoon. It was hard work, but I didn't mind it. In fact, I came to realize that while I needed to work in order to go out and have fun, the work *itself* could be fun too.

After this, I worked as a dishwasher in a Chinese restaurant, a prep chef at a steakhouse, and CFFO (Chief French Fry Officer) at Burger King. The work in the food and beverage business is *tough*. Whether it's the prep station, dish pit, grill, wherever, you have to be cranking out all the time to keep the restaurant running. If you slack off, the whole business grinds to a halt. I think this is where I first learned the importance of systems and critical thinking without even knowing it.

Kitchens are one of the places where people work the hardest. But I enjoyed being in the action like that, and it taught me a level of discipline and focus needed to keep up.

I worked a number of jobs throughout high school. That number is somewhere around 10. And I'm grateful to say I never got fired from any of them—nope, not even the paper route! I also didn't just work in restaurants. Our town has a heavy-duty tourism industry, and I found myself switching into many resort hospitality roles as well.

During summer breaks, I'd work stints as a bellman or desk clerk in one of the many beachfront resorts. This was my first real foray into guest services and gave me the truest taste of what a hospitality career was like. As you can imagine, I *really* enjoyed it. It felt like something I could do, in some way, for my career.

By the time I graduated from Father Lopez Catholic High School in 1976, I wasn't sure what I wanted to do *exactly*, but I knew I wanted to pursue something in the hospitality industry. With this in mind, I ultimately decided to go to Florida State University to study in their hotel restaurant management program. So, up to Tallahassee I went.

By spring of 1978, although I was certain about a career in hospitality, my direction was still unclear and I felt like I needed to step back from school to sort myself out. I came home to talk to my parents about it and see if it would be alright to take a break and start working in hospitality again.

My parents were understanding and agreed that it was probably the best course of action. Of course, they were all about allowing us to find our own paths, but they weren't going to let me get stuck.

"I don't want you thinking that you're going to live in this house for years on end," my dad said, "if you're going to take a break, you're going to do *something*. Why don't you check out that Walt Disney World place in Orlando?"

We'd been to Disney as a family a few times. Back then, there wasn't much west of Orlando proper. I remember my siblings and I having a contest in the back of the station wagon to see who would spot the castle first. I was as familiar with it as the next kid in Central Florida.

Disney isn't too far from Ormond Beach, and it was clearly on its way to becoming the epicenter of hospitality. My dad's suggestion made a lot of sense. In the early summer of 1978, I drove out to Disney and applied to become a cast member. I decided I would get some experience there while

I figured out what I wanted to do. I didn't know it at the time, but I would come to realize that *this* was exactly where I was supposed to be and exactly what I wanted to do. Little did I know, my father's suggestion would chart my course for the next 43 years. Thanks Dad!

Decade I

The timing of everything couldn't have been better—I drove out to apply to be a cast member right when Disney was in a big hiring period to fill summer positions. Not that I was all that aware of staffing logistics back then or anything, but Disney had only a few "peaks" of business during the year: summer, Thanksgiving/Christmas, and Easter. In hindsight, I happened to have gotten to the right place at the right time.

I walked into the casting trailer, filled out an application, and then I was asked to come back the next day. I drove back the next day, and boom! I got the job.

Originally, I was hired to work in Attractions on Main Street, USA. That's where I thought I'd be working on my first day of assignment, but plans changed. I learned in orientation that I was a little bit older than most of the other new cast members. At 20, I was one of the few who could go work in Transportation, so that's where I got reassigned to on Day 2.

Now, I didn't just go anywhere in Transportation. I was moved into the watercraft department. As someone who grew up on the water, I was thrilled. I got to do what I loved for a whopping $3 an hour—what a great gig!

My official watercraft license.

Me piloting the Voyager launch at the Contemporary Resort dock in 1978.

Even before the addition of three more parks and a number of hotels, water parks, and more, Disney had a massive amount of real estate out there. With that much land, you need to have a solid transportation infrastructure to get everyone around. Transportation includes the buses, Monorails, parking, and watercraft vessels that bring guests and cast members to and from everywhere on the property. While my first assignment wasn't inside the Magic Kingdom, it became pretty obvious that I was fortunate to have been placed into a critical support system of the guest experience.

Of course, I wasn't really thinking about all this at 20. I was thinking: *They want to pay me to drive boats all day? Hell yeah!* Watercraft was *the* place to be, but you had to be mature and appreciate the responsibility for what it was—you were operating free-floating vessels loaded with people in any given weather conditions. I had a lot of fun, but I took it as seriously as I could.

There were six different types of watercraft vessels that I could have ultimately been assigned to on any given day. The first, which most guests are familiar with, are the large ferry boats that take guests from the Transportation and Ticket Center to the Magic Kingdom and back. There's also a number of launches and motor cruisers that take guests to the parks. At night, the Electrical Water Pageant was on display for our park and resort guests on Bay Lake and the Seven Seas Lagoon.

It's a big role to be at the wheel like that. Bad weather was bad weather, and I had to learn how to navigate everything from a simple downpour to a tropical storm. But man, it was *fun*. I really enjoyed every part of that adventure.

For my entry into Disney, it was such a cool department to come into. I quickly found a strong sense of community that went far beyond the job. We would all go to the beach, camping, rafting, and a lot of other recreational activities off the clock. Mark Kirchof has been my best buddy for the last four decades and worked with me during this time. He ended up spending his career in the air—first in the Air Force and then as a commercial airlines pilot—but we often reminisce of the wonderful (and crazy) times we had here. Not everyone was a lifer, but it was a welcoming and supportive environment for all while they were there to learn and grow in their own capacities.

It really didn't even feel like "work" in the way that many other people experience their jobs. I was doing something I loved with a great group of people. At some point during that summer, I realized I wanted to stay permanently and pursue a career there.

I'd been initially hired as a CT (casual temporary) part-time summer cast member. As the summer peak wound down into the slower fall period, I was lucky enough to be converted to full-time. Once I was fully "in," the path to moving up became pretty clear—if you were good at what you did, you could take on more responsibilities. These additional responsibilities served as stairsteps of growth into bigger roles. It wasn't long before I started up my own path.

First, I was given the opportunity to be a trainer. This was an as-needed role where I was paid a premium to train new hires at a "life-changing" extra twenty cents per hour, which was big money at the time. From there, I became a lead, which is more or less a shift foreman. Becoming a lead was a big deal and set the stage for whether you could go further. As a lead, I had a lot more responsibilities, but also more visibility to leadership. I was knocking on the door to management potential.

I was working for a lot of great leaders at this time, and this is when the lightbulbs started to pop. I could see who stood out as both influencers and who had earned the respect of the cast members. Of course, there were the leaders who led through intimidation and fear, but they were by far the minority. It became very clear to me in this early stage of my career that, in fact, leadership *and* relationships really did matter. I took the opportunity to observe and learn and apply the traits from these great leaders to develop my own leadership style. Not in any Machivellian way—it wasn't *that* complex or competitive. I just demonstrated that I was capable of taking on more responsibilities and growing further, and that's what happened.

Eventually, I was moved into the upper echelon within the lead position, which was called a Training Lead. This role connected me directly to the supervisor responsible for all training within Watercraft. Part of my responsibilities in this role was to build the training program, operating guides, protocols, all that other minutiae. This gave me more exposure to the role of management and the importance of diversifying my experiences and, when the opportunity arose, was rewarded with a lead position in the Magic Kingdom.

Of course, I'd never worked "in" the park before. I'd also never stepped foot in Attractions before, either. Attractions in Adventureland became my very first experience as a lead within the park. I was assigned to the Enchanted Tiki Room (I was the cast member in the tropical yellow smock who woke up José and the rest of the flock) for about six or so months and really enjoyed working inside the park. And, unbeknownst to me, another major opportunity opened up.

This was just before the time that Epcot Center[1] was announced and ultimately opened. The idea for Epcot came from Walt's last stated vision before passing in 1966, the Experimental Prototype Community of Tomorrow (EPCOT Center), where commerce and communities from around the world would come together to showcase the diversity of products and experiences that, during this era with encyclopedias as the only research reference, provided extraordinary insight to the world at large. While Walt unfortunately passed before this vision could be completed, it eventually became the genesis for the second park on the property.

Another park these days would still be a big deal, but a new, second theme park back then was *huge*—it would quite literally double the size of everything. It was also a much different concept than what people had ever seen before. As this new addition was starting to surface, guests were asking: "Epcot? What's an Epcot?" Everybody knew what a castle was or who Mickey Mouse is, but nobody really knew what an Epcot was. To answer, the theater that ran *The Walt Disney Story* on Main Street was temporarily converted into The Epcot Preview Center in 1980 so guests could visit and be immersed in the new concepts and experiences involved in this new undertaking.

---

1 The park was officially called EPCOT Center until 1994, at which point we started just calling it Epcot. For clarity, we'll refer to it as Epcot from here on out.

So, what'd any of that have to do with me? At this monumentally important time in Disney's history, I found myself on a shortlist of candidates for lead positions who would be assigned to open up the preview center. It goes without saying, but this was a really big deal—I spent a month in special training to get deeply immersed in what this new park was going to be and how it would change the landscape. We got to hear directly from the Imagineers and other inspirational figures about all that this new park had to offer. It was a massive and ambitious expansion, and I was lucky enough to be directly involved in some way.

As Epcot started coming out of the ground, the infrastructure had to also get built up to support it. That need is what created my first salaried management assignment as a temporary Assistant Transportation Supervisor in the peak summer period of 1982. Specifically, I was part of the leadership team that was tasked with running parking operations for Epcot's opening.

It might not sound as exciting as driving boats or working directly in the park, but Transportation was just as fun and an important role. By "important," I really mean it's absolutely critical for everything to function—after all, it's what connects the magic. My time in Transportation gifted me with a number of important learning experiences that impacted me for the rest of my career.

First, I got to work with a whole different kind of crowd. Transportation has older, more seasoned cast members, something I wasn't used to before. I also got to see the full scope of the property and all the moving parts of Transportation, which is truly mind-blowing.

Transportation was also a great reminder that we live in the real world, and we have to pay attention to the real-world safety of our guests and cast members. When you're dealing with free-floating vessels, multiple buses on the roadways, monorails, and parking trams, you come to realize how important our focus on safety truly is. We call Disney "the most magical place on Earth," but there's a mantra we say even more often: "Safety begins with me...no one gets hurt." Regardless of whether we're running rides, serving food in a restaurant, moving people via transportation, etcetera, we are here to give guests an incredible experience, but we also have their lives in our hands every minute of every day. That can never be forgotten, and that's why safety is one of the most important of the Four (now Five) Keys.

That's not to say that every minute of every day couldn't also be a great time, too. I was always focused on doing a great job and having fun doing it. And there was a *lot* to do there—Transportation was a huge part of the growth and expansion that had to happen to support Epcot. We contributed to the opening's success through the new logistics and operation of everything in our department.

I was specifically in parking, which is often overlooked. There's a real science to parking that a lot of people don't seem to understand. Things would get very messy, very quickly if everyone parked their car wherever. All the guests driving onto the property need to be directed in a clear, organized, and safe way. Smooth parking operations were a critical part of handling the rising attendance numbers.

Parking operations also contributed to the successful opening of Epcot on October 1st, 1982, 11 years to the date after the Magic Kingdom. We had just begun operation of the new toll plaza and parking lots for the opening day, and we were all so geared up for guests to come. I remember being in the parking lot when the first car came rolling in around 2 am. The energy of everyone—cast members and guests—was something you could feel in the air.

Opening days are typically filled with grand opening ceremonies and other entertainment. I was just outside the turnstiles when they brought the First Family into the park and awarded them lifetime passes. Then, all the guests entered, and it was an incredible hubbub of music and activities all day. Transportation may have been working on the outskirts of all this, but we were sucked into the excitement too. After all, we were all working together, regardless of our day jobs, to deliver excellence, especially during this significant milestone.

After the success of Epcot's opening, my temporary management position was converted to a permanent one and I was brought into the park as the Assistant Supervisor for Attractions in the World Showcase.

To fully fulfill Walt's vision of bringing commerce and communities together, Epcot is divided into two distinct lands: Future World and the World Showcase. Future World represents the commerce side, while the World Showcase represents the communities. Described as the "1.2 mile walk around the world," it's a key piece of creating the interconnected world that Walt had envisioned within the park.

Each pavilion is designed to depict a distinct country—Mexico, Norway, China, Germany, Italy, the United States, Japan, France, the United Kingdom, Canada, and later Morocco as well—as authentically as possible. Guests can go inside any restaurants, theaters, attractions, and shops within that area and see things that represent each culture. As part of that effort, we had the exciting task of staffing the pavilions with cultural students from each country to really bring it to life.

Our International Program allows students to come here on a special work visa, live in cast member housing, and work for about a year. It's a great win-win: they get a valuable experience abroad and the opportunity to represent their country, and we are able to inject the personal authenticity into each pavilion that we couldn't in any other way.

Aside from all my other assignments associated with the role, recruiting and leading our international team was one of the best parts of it. I had never been exposed to so many cultures before. You could smell the variety just by walking into the breakroom where all the cast members ate their meals. I even had the opportunity to go on a few recruiting trips abroad. It was a really, really neat learning experience on diversity that's shaped my leadership to this day.

The diversity of the World Showcase was a large part of fulfilling Walt's vision, but the technology implemented in Future World was just as big. We had a lot of things that were forward-thinking and unique for the time.

If you can, think about what it was like back then. Technologically as we know it today didn't really exist. Smartphones, laptops, and widespread Internet usage was still decades away. Leadership at my level communicated by writing messages in our logbooks. The most "tech" thing we had was beepers—you could leave a message to someone, and they'd call you back on a landline. That was where we were at.

Future World was all about showcasing the latest and greatest in developments, so innovative technology came to the forefront in a variety of ways here. One of the best examples of this was the World Key Information System. Epcot is known for its many unique and top-tier dining destinations, and it started off strong with that. But with all the restaurants and no pre-arrival procedure for booking them, guests needed some way to make reservations while they were in the park. That's where the World Key came in.

There were numerous kiosks inside the post-show area of SpaceShip Earth. Guests could walk up to any one of them to speak with an agent over video call to make reservations. Remember, this was long before Zoom ever became a thing. Getting to engage with someone face-to-face on a screen was pretty advanced for the time.

Technology was not only used as a logistical tool to support the guest experience, but also for storytelling. To name just one thing, *The American Adventure* in the United States pavilion relies on technology to maintain the integrity of its storytelling. When you peel it back, there's a staggering amount of technology supporting everything—the sets rising up and coming down, the moving carriages, the many choreographed Audio-Animatronics—involved with running the show. Technology allows this all to happen seamlessly.

Technology also enables guests to be immersed in the experience. If you saw, say, all the gears inside of Mark Twain's Audio-Animatronic or the mechanics of the stage floor, you'd be taken out of the story. But you don't—you get taken through the history of the United States by the people within it. The bubble of Disney magic never pops. And that's amazing.

The opening of Epcot represented a new chapter at Disney, but we experienced even more change within its first few years. In 1984, Michael Eisner was appointed CEO, which led to a huge shift in the energy and focus of the entire organization. The start of the Eisner era was marked by an attempted hostile takeover on top of the turmoil of new leadership, so tensions were running high. While those of us on the front lines couldn't quite grasp the magnitude of this change, I could definitely feel the trade winds shifting. Change was coming.

With change, of course, always comes some fear. The rumor mill ran abound. I remember one particularly dark day when everyone was saying—though nobody could confirm—that there would be mass layoffs the next day. It was nerve-wracking coming into work not knowing if my job was on the line. People were scared, and there was much speculation on what would happen.

Under Michael Eisner and Frank Wells's leadership, the tides turned quickly and there was a very strong focus in bringing all aspects of the company's assets together, which brought the word "synergy" to life. Under Eisner, the silos we'd previously worked in were broken down and brought together. This was apparent even at my generally low level of salaried leadership—going forward, we were operating as one organization rather than as a series of self-contained groups.

This was a big change for *everyone*. There was a lot of movement of a lot of people into new roles and responsibilities, me included. While I had already worked plenty of different jobs by that point (and by the end of my career, my guesstimate is that I had about 26 different roles within the organization), this was when I really started to move around like a hot potato in the different lines of business.

First, I was reassigned to the main entrance operation at the Magic Kingdom. The focus of the main entrance was primarily on guest relations and vacation planning, which meant a heavy focus on ticket sales. I'd never been so close to the money side of the organization before, so it was an interesting experience to see the nuts and bolts of the cash flow.

I was only there for about six months when I got a call from Greg Emmer, a highly respected leader who had just taken on the additional responsibility of Entertainment, asking me to join him in the Entertainment organization. Unlike many of my other assignments, this was a very different move.

Entertainment produced the parades, shows, character appearances, and other famous productions within the parks. It was also a silo they wanted to bring closer in the goal of creating continuity across all lines of business. Moving me, an Operations guy, into Entertainment was one small piece of a larger strategy to connect the two departments together.

It was a big challenge to be welcomed as someone who didn't grow up in Entertainment. I couldn't dance. (Still can't.) I couldn't sing. (Still can't.) I couldn't do any of that stuff. What I *could* do was build relationships. And while of course I didn't necessarily realize it at the time, relationships are the bridges that bring previously disparate organization cultures together, united toward a more common vision. This was my first true test in understanding relationships and the importance of connecting within a completely different culture. It was also a lesson in humility—I was totally out of my area here, and I had to have the vulnerability to admit it. I appreciated their expertise and approached them authentically, and that's how I eventually cracked the shell.

Really, it was a lot of fun. After all, it's not called "Entertainment" for nothing. I got to work directly with the characters and learn just how important they are for the guest experience. As part of the newly-aggressive marketing efforts, I also went out on what we called "character cavalcade trips." To bring people to Disney, we brought Disney to the people—we'd take characters into public places like malls and hospitals to hold meet-and-greets and sometimes even put on remote stage shows with singers and dancers from the Magic Kingdom.

These trips meant that I got to travel to many cities in the US and Canada—Montreal, Ottawa, Toronto, Miami, Philadelphia, New York, just to name a few. I also got to do a lot of other cool stuff like flying on Walt's two-prop plane, the corporate jet back in the day, and waterskiing with Donald and Goofy on Bay Lake. As wild as that sounds, I've got the pictures to prove it.

Taking off to the Midwest with the Fab Five (Minnie is already in the pilot seat).

My two-year run in Entertainment came to an end when I was promoted to Area Manager of Main Street. An Area Manager is essentially a department head with several Assistant Supervisors underneath them. As the name suggests, I was responsible for the entirety of the Main Street area. This included guest relations, main entrance operations, the castle hub, and everything else. It was my first "leader of leaders" assignment, an exciting milestone in my career.

The new paradigm shift toward synergy and proactive marketing had started to really kick in during this time. Park anniversaries, giveaways, and other promotions were driving demand and incremental attendance. We were giving guests as many reasons to attend as possible. Simultaneously, the organization was working to connect film production and the parks more strongly together. The dots were getting connected in a big way.

They decided to take this connection even further—what if the movies could come to life in the parks? This premise became the third park on the property, Disney-MGM Studios[2].

At this point, I'd started to realize that being on the front lines of innovative experiences was appealing to me. I was drawn to the new and creative things coming out of the organization, and I really wanted to be a part of the progress in some way. I talked to my leader to see if I could join the opening team.

---

2 As of 2008, the park is now called Disney's Hollywood Studios.

My role in the opening turned out to be...wait for it...in bus operations. It's not exactly the role that I sought out, but any role in Transportation was formative in continuing to expand my visibility and awareness of the total property size and scale. I was responsible for leading cast members within this part of Transportation as we expanded the bus fleet, mapped new routes, and worked out the logistics ahead of the opening. Once again, I was outside of the turnstiles on opening day.

The opening of Disney-MGM Studios on May 1st, 1989 marked the beginning of what Eisner declared would be a period of massive expansion across all areas of the organization. The Disney Decade really turned out to be a great growth spurt for us. The development and expansion of our property was about to reach new heights, and I was more than ready for it.

Decade II

If I had to use one word to describe the response to Disney-MGM's opening, it'd be this—underestimated. This was Eisner's first "fingerprint" in the parks, and he wanted to create something smaller and more intimate compared to the expansiveness of, say, Epcot. While I wasn't privy to any conversations, I'm sure the size was also in part to minimize potential risks with cannibalizing our attendance and directly competing with the forthcoming Universal Studios.

Either way, Disney-MGM Studios was first created as what others called a "half-day" park. It was designed to accommodate a much smaller attendance base than the Magic Kingdom or Epcot could. In hindsight, this design concept was an example of us talking to ourselves. Guests have high expectations for Disney parks and experiences, and the Studios delivered on them just like all the others. So, it became clear very early on that demand far exceeded its original design. The Studios was proof that if you build it, they will come.

I got to see this for myself both in my Transportation role and when I was moved into the park as Area Manager of Main Entrance Operations. I mean, that's as up-close as you can get. For that first year, we were at capacity more often than not. But you can't pack the place to the gills—safety is always at the forefront, not ticket sales. Especially during this time, we were hypervigilant about managing the number of guests inside the park.

Mind you, we didn't have a reservation system back then. When it came to predicting each day's potential attendance, previous arrival patterns were the closest thing we had to a crystal ball. Yesterday's actuals informs today's potentials. We also took turnstile counts about every hour and kept watch of the arrival pipeline, which is all the guests coming into the toll plaza, riding a bus, etcetera. When we began to reach capacity, we would make the ultimate closing call based on how many were in the park and in the pipeline. It was a big valve to shut off, so we had to do it right.

And it was all the time. From our perspective, every day felt like a peak holiday. While we did what we could at the entrance, there was only one way we could accommodate the sky-high attendance—expand, expand, expand.

Disney-MGM Studios essentially doubled in size within its first five years. Backstage areas, or areas blocked off from guests and pedestrian thoroughfare, became onstage areas. Places like Mickey's Avenue and New York Street were not originally a part of the park, but they were incorporated into the guest areas to keep up with the need. New experiences and attractions like Mickey's Avenue, The Tower of Terror, and the *Beauty and the Beast* stage show on Sunset Boulevard were also added to increase the park's offerings. Really, I would say the opening wasn't complete until about 5 years later because of the constant expansion.

The first few years were all about closely controlling the park's capacity and leading the park through significant growth just to handle the demand. After that, day-to-day operations began to stabilize. Hopefully that all didn't sound too grueling—it was pretty crazy, but it was also one of the more exciting roles in my career. The team I worked with was wildly creative with an entrepreneurial streak—Bruce Laval was the park's VP and brought extraordinary intelligence and insight, Bob Lamb was the GM and incredibly creative and competitive, John Phelan brought amazing energy and creativity to the mix, and Phil Holmes was my peer in running Operations inside the park. Phil and I would go on to work closely together throughout our careers and is a dear friend today.

In the park with Phil Holmes in the middle, John Phelan on the right, and Donald Duck wearing a sombrero in the back.

From top to bottom, there was a level of organizational vibrancy unique to this leadership team. Something about the Studios had a competitive spirit to it. Perhaps because we had beat out Universal Studios in the arms race to open first, but everyone was always looking to try new and innovative things. This, of course, was right up my alley. We might've made it through the expansion, but we weren't ready to put our feet up.

Before I get into how we inadvertently created a startup within the organization, and while there are many examples to share, allow me to provide a little background context for our focus on optimizing our use of the theme park itself during non-traditional hours. At the time, Disney hosted large corporate events in properties outside of the parks. These events, while impressive, were also unnecessarily expensive for the organization, given that we often recreated theme park environments in convention ballrooms. It had to have been a pain to replicate Main Street, USA in the ballroom of the Contemporary Resort, and it wasn't cheap either.

One day, I was sitting around in Bob Lamb's office (if you look up "Make Work Fun" in the dictionary, you'll see his picture) with Phil Holmes, John Phelan, and Barry Carlson, all representing our various disciplines, when we started ideating on bringing convention group events to life in the park. The team got to thinking—instead of burning resources to recreate the parks, why not host the events here? If the parks are just sitting there unused after hours, we couldn't find any reason not to.

While the corporations would still hold their daytime activities in the hotels, we came up with themed events to host at night in the Studios. We'd have a welcome ticker-tape parade, open attractions, and deliver really unique dining experiences like dinner right outside the Great Movie Ride's courtyard or on the set of the Indiana Jones's Epic Stunt Spectacular...stuff you couldn't do when the park was usually open. Needless to say, it was a ton of fun, and it pulled the various lines of business together in a very unique way.

And by leveraging the park assets that were otherwise dormant at the end of the day, we generated a massive amount of extra revenue on top of our daily cash flow that we hadn't really planned for. Instead of simply closing the park and shutting down for the day, we could now pivot into event mode and keep the Operations (and high-margin revenue) flowing.

These after-hours events took off exponentially, and we only grew it from there. We went from an occasional event to a *lot*, fast. I started to take on increasing responsibilities—first by developing the sales packages and creating brochures, before eventually being reassigned full-time as the Operations Manager for Parks Special Events.

In this role, I was able to pull together a small but mighty team—Tracy Donaldson, Kim Wilson Hayek, Kim Warsicki, among others—and working hand-in-hand with our sales partners, we pulled these sales packages together and brought them to life in all parks. This new area focus allowed me to grow into my first executive position as General Manager of DEG (Disney Events Groups). I led the team to get Special Events running in all parks and connected to sales.

I was in a really cool position where we worked toward full optimization of our resources. To clear out the park at the end of the operating day without inconveniencing our guests and then offer it up again was truly making use of our assets and real estate in the best way possible. It was great to stay with this from the beginning as basically a startup idea all the way to scaling it across the parks. In hindsight, this was my first major experience with optimization, something I continued to hone in on throughout my career.

It wasn't all sunshine though. I believe that in life, you have four distinct circles: faith (connection to some higher purpose, meaning of life type stuff), family (how you're doing as a spouse, sibling, parent, whatever), career (performance and professional fulfillment), and social (friends are important too). To live well, you need to balance these circles in good harmony.

You can usually live mostly okay with one circle off-kilter. Two pose a threat to your life's balance. If three are off, you really need to take a step back and evaluate what's going on as soon as possible or you are *screwed*.

Well, primarily due to personal reasons, virtually all of my freaking circles were a bit out of whack here, and it was an important time for me to reassess my priorities at work and at play, and get focused on my next chapters.

My general disorientation was for many different reasons, but the crux of the matter was this—while I was proud of what we had created and did well in the sales arena, it's not where my passion was. In my heart of hearts, I knew I wanted to get back to Operations and drive significant value in new and unique ways.

The timing here, at least, was good—I needed a change right when the organization was set to announce the opening of the fourth park, Disney's Animal Kingdom, a concept entirely different from anything we had ever done before. I went into Bruce Laval's office and asked to be a part of the opening team.

Bruce was the head of all Operations and the creator of FastPass. He instilled in many of us the true balance of art and science well before I started to call it that and was an extraordinarily strategic leader whom I admired greatly. Thankfully, this particular dream of joining the opening team came true.

Within a month, I was assigned to be the GM of Operations at Animal Kingdom. Aside from the Magic Kingdom, I've been involved with every park's opening in some way, but this was the first time where I was there early—three years before opening! I realized I would be a part of the formation of this new and exciting fourth theme park. With my incredible team at the ready, we helped build and open the park from the Operations perspective, and it was an honor to contribute to development at this level.

Animal Kingdom was a profoundly new concept because, for the first time ever, we were building a park where animals of all types would play an incredible role in the story arc. But we didn't want it to be perceived as just a zoo or another "typical" theme park with some live animal gimmick—we wanted to tell stories of animals both real, imaginary, and extinct, and we wanted to incorporate the animals and the lands they come from directly into the storytelling, with a strong call to action for conservation and wildlife preservation.

It's unlike the way technology is incorporated into the storytelling of the parks. Technology is utilized to maintain the story's integrity and allow guests to stay immersed within the magic. Here, live animals *are* the story. I mean, Kilimanjaro Safaris would just be a drive if it weren't for the African wildlife you might see along the way. Nature walks without wildlife would just be, well...walks. All the creatures and critters within the park are what make it *Animal* Kingdom, after all.

We were looking to build a park that provided top-quality care for the animals, showcased their geographic areas of origin, and emphasized the theme of conservation throughout. This was no small task, and it took a large team of all kinds of expertise to bring it to life.

Of course, I don't have to tell you it was also wildly fun. Many of those who joined the leadership team for opening had come over from the Studios, and they brought that same liveliness here too. I was back in my element of Operations and I got to travel all over the place. I visited the Imagineers in California multiple times to share Operational design criteria and give input toward development. Like Epcot, we wanted to bring authenticity to the places we showcased, so I also went on recruiting trips in Africa—Botswana, Nairobi, Johannesburg and Cape Town in South Africa, etcetera—to hire cultural representatives for the park. It was incredible to watch the park build up out of the ground like this.

The unique challenge here was that we were bringing in animals from all over the world to Walt Disney World, and we needed to design the environment as much like their natural habitats as possible. The health and happiness of the animals were, of course, top priority. To ensure their wellbeing, the organization brought in over 300 zoological professionals from around the world. One of them was my future wife, Marty.

Marty initially came to help create the *Flights of Wonder* stage show in the Caravan Theater. We first met at the Contemporary Resort when we were ideating various stage show concepts. Marty was working as a consultant for a third-party show producer and was brought in to contribute to this ideation session.

I was immediately struck by Marty. She had a strong sense of bravery and an innately creative mindset. Marty didn't care about anybody's title in the room—her focus was clearly set on creating excellence by leveraging her animal husbandry experience. Marty, as it turns out, was also struck by me. She later told me she knew we were going to get married the day we met. But, we didn't have the opportunity to connect until about a year later.

Marty was eventually hired as the Curator of Behavioral Husbandry at Animal Kingdom and moved here permanently. We started dating about six months after that and married in the fall of 1999. And, here we are today.

By the way, Marty's work is incredibly cool...and complex. She helped create the animal enrichment and training programs for the zookeepers to use with the many species there. Just to give you one out of many examples, she can train a rhino to present their *derriere* for a shot. How badass is that?!

Animal Kingdom opened on Earth Day in 1998 to an overwhelmingly positive reception. Our focus for that first year was dialing in on scale and getting Operations running smoothly. This was especially important because it opened with a provocative new organization structure, something different than what the other parks had.

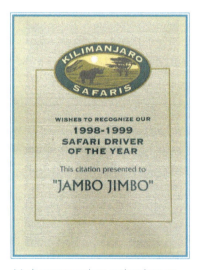

My honorary plaque that hangs in Tusker House Restaurant in Harambe Village at Disney's Animal Kingdom.

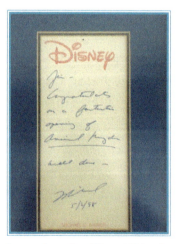

A note I received from Michael Eisner after the park's opening.

Standing with the first prototype of the Kilimanjaro Safaris ride vehicle.

This plaque was made by Jeff Vahle and the FOS (Facilities Operations Services) team at Disney's Animal Kingdom. The Mickey shape is made from actual cement pucks taken from the Kilimanjaro Safaris ride path.

Disney's Animal Kingdom opening leadership team.

Before diving into the structure, I do want to mention that many of the opening team members of Animal Kingdom ended up becoming the "Who's Who" in the Leadership Hall of Fame. Most members of the opening team, as well as those who followed thereafter, springboarded into bigger leadership roles over the years. Why? Wait for it...because we Engaged, Inspired, and Led—each other AND our teams. The DNA and culture we built were formative for me and several others, and I feel I learned so much about who I wanted to be as a leader in this assignment. This Hall of Fame included: Bruce Laval, Bob Lamb, Beth Stevens, Erin Wallace, Jeff Vahle, Debbie DeMars, Trevor Larsen, Joe Schott, Val Bunting, Jackie Ogden, Donald Brannon, Tim Sypko, Kevin Lansberry, Michael Colglazier, Josh D'Amaro, Djuan Rivers, Phil Holmes, among others.

We normally had what's called the "Matrix Model." In the Matrix Model, vertical lines of business (Food and Beverage, Merchandise, Entertainment, Attractions, etcetera) are run separately while the horizontal lines (executives and leaders) focus on development, optimization, and standardization.

MATRIX MODEL

	Magic Kingdom	Epcot	Hollywood Studios	Animal Kingdom
Entertainment				
Merchandise				
Food and Beverage				

In the Proprietor Model, you have a GM responsible for each land and everything in it. They were responsible for all lines of business within their area, but they had a team of direct reports who provided their respective line of business expertise. We wanted to create an ownership mindset within the leaders, and the model definitely helped the GMs feel their footprint to the fullest extent.

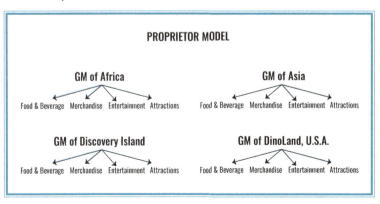

BACKGROUND 41

We were able to do this at the time because we were empowered to think about different organizational structures rather than maintaining consistency across all of the parks. It was a new way of doing things that brought the different lines of business together and got the GMs to lead holistically. I was the architect of this concept, so I could be biased, but it shook things up in a really good way. There's a lot to unpack here—the end-to-end experience, Mastery and Command, thinking holistically, optimization versus transformation, etcetera—so we'll get more into all this later on.

Marty and I were married at Disney's Wedding Pavilion, and our wedding reception was the very first one held at Typhoon Lagoon. It was a great time—arriving guests checked their dress shoes at the door and donned a personalized pair of flip-flops enroute to an incredible beach setting and clambake feast.

Photo from our wedding reception at Typhoon Lagoon. Note the surfboard in the back.

We began our lives together on the Clermont chain of lakes, continuing our mutual passion for water activities. Shortly after we got settled in, I got a call from a senior leader in California with the offer to join the opening team for the next new thing—Disney's California Adventure in Anaheim, directly adjacent to the Magic Kingdom park where it all began in 1955. This offer was also a huge promotional opportunity, since I'd be moving from a GM role to a VP. But, it also meant we would have to move all the way out to California.

Marty and I had just bought our home in Clermont, so the idea of uprooting our lives wasn't exactly great. But I was always interested in these new adventures, and the California site was in need of some seasoned people to help with opening the new park. Keep in mind, this was their first time doing that, so some experienced people from the WDW site would greatly aid with it. After some consideration, we decided that I'd accept the job.

I was the first to move out there in the spring of 2000. Marty followed some months later. Although the move was difficult, it was still an exciting time. I was one of the first people to "cross-pollinate" and gain work experience at both of our domestic sites. While there were many challenges both personally and professionally with this move, it would turn out to be an incredible catalyst for broader thinking beyond one single site.

There was a lot of change happening—a new millenium, new park, new job, new city. As we started the new millennium on the other side of the country, change would only continue for the organization, the nation, and for our own family, too.

Decade III

The move to California was complicated not only by the fact that Marty and I had just gotten married and bought our house in Clermont, but since Marty was continuing her efforts at Animal Kingdom during a crucial time, she couldn't leave as quickly as I could. So, I went out to California about six months ahead of Marty while she wrapped things up back in Orlando.

In that interim, I lived in an apartment only a few hundred yards from several of SoCal's legendary surf breaks. I got to take my longboard out and hit the surf in my offtime, which was a bit of a dream come true for me—I grew up reading about the waves on the West Coast in *Surfer* magazine.

There's a huge difference between the surf on the East and West Coast. For one, it's *way* colder—as a Florida boy, I had to adjust to wearing a wetsuit like 90% of the time. The East's is also driven by the finicky nature of storms, whereas the West's is driven by the comparatively steadier swells in the ocean. The surf out there is consistently bigger and more powerful. Every East Coast surfer dreams of going to the West Coast.

After Marty made the move, we bought a newly-built home in Laguna Niguel, a stellar location just a few miles inland from Laguna Beach *and* overlooking Saddleback Mountain, and settled in once again. We were in a very new and different environment, but I was doing one of the things I knew best—opening new parks.

The expansion of Disneyland Resort with the addition of Disney's California Adventure was a big bet—there was some concern the California theme *in* California wouldn't be as broadly appealing for guests, especially for local Californians. So while its potential popularity may have seemed like a dice roll, its initial opening on February 8th in 2001 turned out to be a success. But the park was really significant in what it did for the organization as a whole.

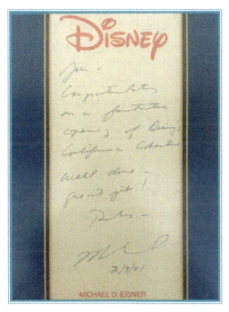

A note I received from Michael Eisner after the opening of Disney's California Adventure.

Like I've said, Disneyland is obviously a landmark destination as the first place where Disney's theme parks came to life, but their leadership had limited experience in opening new parks. The team over at WDW had four park openings under our belt at this point, so that's why some of us were brought over to help contribute to this opening. While it wasn't previously unheard of, this was one of the first instances of pulling people together across sites in such a way.

Prior to this, there wasn't much connectivity between the sites. California, Florida, Paris, and Tokyo ran more or less as standalones. This was one of the events that started to tie the parks and personnel together, and they have only further connected as we continued to open more sites around the world.

The opening of Disney's California Adventure became the tipping point that turned Disneyland from a single park into a full-fledged resort destination. While it was only across the promenade of the original park, it really did double the size of the site in the same way that Epcot did at WDW. It was a pretty monumental thing to be a part of.

But, there's also no place like home. As much as I appreciated the adventure into a new territory, the experience also made Marty and I realize that Orlando and, therefore, Walt Disney World, was really where we were supposed to be, particularly in light of the events that would unfold as a result of the 9/11 attacks, which reshaped operational protocols for all of our parks and led to many other changes within the organization. So when I got offered the opportunity to come back to base shortly after opening, we took it.

Opening a second theme park at Disneyland, where it all began in 1955, was an incredible experience and we were once again successful in bringing this new product to life. However, from a leadership perspective, there's a lot more drama and timing to this story that I'm not going to get into here—in some cases, I witnessed the dark side of very senior leadership (or, lack of) and was reminded of the importance of leadership experience, credibility, and integrity.

Suffice to say, Marty and I clicked the heels of our red slippers, closed our eyes, and chanted, "There's no place like home, there's no place like home..." Soliciting a return to Orlando was a big ask, especially in the aftermath of 9/11. To this day, I'm eternally grateful to Al Weiss, Lee Cockerell, Karl Holz, and especially Erin Wallace for the opportunity to return home.

Although we were excited to come home, our move back was about to be complex. When we had started our lives in California, we had also decided to start our family too. After we realized we had some challenges with doing so naturally, some very close friends who had traveled the path recommended we try in vitro fertilization. They introduced us to their doctor, and so we went that route.

So, we found out that Marty was pregnant around the same time we decided to go back. We also found out that we weren't expecting just one. I remember the doctor telling us at the first appointment that we were having twins, which was pretty cool, especially considering that my sister Kathy and I are also twins.

As it turns out, we weren't really having twins. The doctor pointed out an "area of suspicion" at the second ultrasound. Well, that area of suspicion was actually Anna! We were having triplets.

Of course, we were a bit shocked by the fact that we were having three kids at once. The surprise was written on our faces—I remember a woman at the post office even asking if we were alright later that day. You could say we were perhaps expecting more than we had expected!

This pregnancy was already complicated given our stage in life, and carrying triplets made it tumultuous. Her doctors advised that she needed to get stabilized before making the move back. So this time, I returned to Orlando first in March of 2002 while Marty stayed near the high-risk pregnancy specialists in California.

I flew back every other week to accompany Marty to the appointments until they gave her the all-clear to come back home about two months later. Our children—Anna, Carter, and JJ—were born at 26 weeks on September 12th, 2002. None of them weighed more than two pounds at birth. JJ's full name was James Duncan MacPhee the Fourth. He passed away from an infection at three weeks old. It goes without saying, but losing a child is an absolutely devastating thing that no parent should ever have to experience. Anna and Carter came home after spending their first three months of their lives in the NICU at AdventHealth.

But there were some bright spots in the midst of this darkness—Marty's incredible strength to carry our children through such a difficult pregnancy, a great medical team that cared for them in their fragile conditions, and the support of all our friends and family.

Anna and Carter's first Christmas.

Walking in Dad's footsteps.

I returned to Walt Disney World as the Director of Park Operations Line of Business. All of the parks were back on the Matrix Structure during this time, and leadership was focused on creating a centralized organization for each line of business—Merchandise, Food and Beverage, and Entertainment. Park Operations was the last line of business formed, and needed someone with experience to help lead it. Coincidentally, I had the experience and was one of the few individuals who had worked on both coasts, so it made sense for me to step into this role.

Park Operations Line of Business was a small but mighty team focused on consistency and standardization of the operating practices and metrics for the site. We were taking the horizontal view of our Operations—looking at development, the long-term masterplan, and how to run our business more effectively and efficiently. Standardization and efficiency were especially important in the post-9/11 era, as it took a while for our business to rebound.

But in this tighter team, leadership had decided not to respond to the panic with major layoffs. We were instead going to take this time to break down, rebuild, and strive toward further continuity between the sites. Unbeknownst to us, we were about to hit a major growth spurt as an organization, so this all worked out in a big way later on.

Working within the centralized line of business is nothing like running the day-to-day stuff. We had to define the standard way of doing things (safety protocols, key performance measurements and metrics, etcetera) while still allowing the room needed for each site to be unique. We found out quickly that if you're too prescriptive, you kill creativity, but if you leave people to their own devices, chaos ensues. Standardization and consistency is a tricky balance to meet here.

I would always refer to it as "pushing a wet noodle." Since we couldn't allow people to do their own thing all of the time, some perceived us as being somewhat monolithic and controlling. The nature of a Matrix-style organization will inevitably create tension, but I think that tension can be healthy to keep people connected to and aligned with the same operating protocols.

I stayed within this role for about four years, which I think back as a great pit stop both professionally and personally—I got to work a more balanced work week while Marty and I got settled back in Orlando with the kids, and my team got to develop leadership expectations and standards that became critical in the coming years. It was a great role to come home to. Then, in 2006, I was offered a different kind of homecoming.

The then-VP of Epcot announced his retirement for April of 2007. Erin Wallace called me when Marty and I were in the Bahamas at a friend's wedding and asked if I wanted to replace him upon his departure, which was an easy and immediate "Yes!" from me. That May, I moved laterally into the role as VP of Epcot and led a team of over seven thousand cast members at Walt's final stated vision...Epcot.

Marty was the one that actually called this role out as a "homecoming" for me, and she was absolutely right. To step in to be the leader of Epcot was an absolutely incredible dream come true. Epcot's always had a special place in my heart.

Given the fact that Epcot had opened 25 years prior and the site's focus was on continued broad-scale expansion, it was time to shift the focus back on revitalizing the park. Epcot was in need of some refresh and, coincidentally, we had new product planned on the short-term horizon to do that. However, we needed to leverage that to turn around the downslide in the metrics. As it turned out, the 25th anniversary served as a fantastic catalyst to turn things around.

Now, that might seem like the no-brainer way to generate excitement and inject some enthusiasm back into Epcot. What could be an easier way to get guests in the park than to celebrate something as significant as its 25th? Well, I was surprisingly a contrarian here.

Because of the DNA of thinking under a "One Disney" mindset, over time, we had shifted away from celebrating individual milestones, so celebrating park anniversaries were not necessarily in vogue. Additionally, the decision has already been made and communicated that we would not be doing a public, guest-facing 25th anniversary celebration. It'd been stated there would be a private, backstage moment to honor the 10/1 anniversary three months beforehand in the summer, but that'd be it.

Well, this just didn't sit right with me, and it continued to fester in my head big-time. It was shaping up to be more of a funeral than a celebration! When the HR specialist came into my office to review the plans for this reverent backstage moment in July, that was enough to put me over the edge. Remember, the anniversary is October 1st—and we were thinking of celebrating it in the *summer*?! I noticed he had a wedding ring. I asked him when his wedding anniversary was, which was in March.

"So when do you and your wife celebrate it?" I asked him.

"Well, on the date of our anniversary." He said.

"So if your anniversary was in October, would you celebrate it with a private, backstage moment in June?"

That's exactly what we were trying to do here, and it wasn't right. Our guests thought so, too. Out of all four parks, Epcot fans are arguably the most purist. They're very passionate and, consequently, *very* opinionated. They were asking what we would be doing for the milestone, and I had no answer for them. It was frankly pretty embarrassing.

One day, I received a call from a 15-year-old fan—his name is Adam Roth and he grew up to work for Disney Cruise Lines—who basically said, "Hey, I'm leading Celebration 25[3], and we're doing something for the anniversary if you'd like to join us." This was so bass ackwards! The fanbase shouldn't be driving the anniversary—that was our job, and we weren't doing it.

---

3 This was a club for the fan-led celebration of the 25th anniversary.

The idea of our fans celebrating an anniversary that we chose to ignore is what finally got us to swing the pendulum and say, "We have to take advantage of the 25th anniversary." I told Adam that we, the organization, would do it with them. There would be a celebration after all.

We decided that we would do a tribute that Epcot deserved. As part of the leadup, we created a modest attraction modeled after the Epcot Preview Center that allowed guests to experience some of the history of Epcot over the 25 years it'd been open. We also put out retro guide maps showing what Epcot looked like on its opening day and took down the 2000 wand on Spaceship Earth (thank you Jeff Vahle), which purists appreciated quite a bit. Our anniversary celebration revitalized the energy at Epcot for guests and cast members alike.

Retro guidemap made to celebrate the 25th Anniversary.

Celebrating the anniversary.

During the 25th Anniversary ceremony at the fountain stage.

With Adam and the late Marty Sklar, a legendary Imagineer who worked with Walt himself. (Photo courtesy of Adam.)

With Adam Roth in front of Spaceship Earth. (Photo courtesy of Adam.)

Ultimately, it was the much-needed rally cry that paid off big time—attendance and guest satisfaction rose, our team got a lot of credit from the fanbase for moving the park to its original state, and corporate allocated more funds to put back into the park. The anniversary, along with new product now preparing to open, attendance and guest satisfaction reversed itself and improved dramatically. Clearly, we must have done something right. Our success broke down the philosophy of not honoring individual milestones, as the other parks have since celebrated their major anniversaries.

Leading Epcot was one of the happiest times of my career. In this role, I met folks who were extremely talented in all facets of the business and would go on to be lifelong business partners and friends—Melissa Valiquette, Natalie Sirianni, Sheri Torres, Wende Bendik, just to name a few. We had so much excitement coming off of the anniversary and had begun to drive the park back to peak performance levels. I was happy and comfortable in the role. Really, I thought to myself that I could stay there for the rest of my career. But as Walt said, "In this volatile business of ours, we can ill afford to rest on our laurels, even to pause in retrospect." And shame on me, because I would have done just that.

Well, there were other cards at play here. Soon after the anniversary, I was tapped to be part of what would become the Next Generation Experience. There are moments in our lives and careers that end up shaping who we are and how we do things, and this was one of them. NGE was one of those pivotal defining moments that would change the culture and fabric of what we do—it innovated the Disney experience, transformed many facets of how the parks run, paved the way for the rest of my career, and established the DNA of my leadership.

The Next Generation Experience

In leading a large-scale business like Walt Disney World, focusing on delivering the base AND maintaining an eye on the future is the foundation of everything we do. Invariably, this means that change is a constant in our organization—across our parks, our product, and our leadership. In 2006, our site leadership changed when Meg Crofton was appointed President of Walt Disney World, the first woman to take on that role. Authentic and true in everything she does, Meg is a master class study on engagement, inspiration, and leadership.

Part of her responsibilities as president was to shape the strategic roadmap for the site, which usually consists of annual business plan reviews (site strategies, key areas of focus, etcetera) and the 10-year capital plan, which is a multi-billion dollar investment model for new attractions, hotels, restaurants, and other new experiences of the brick-and-mortar variety. She and the senior leadership team went out to California to present all of this, which was all very important and part of the overall strategic direction of the site.

Around the same time as the presentation, the Chairman had been flipping through an issue of *O Magazine* when he found a troubling stat—according to the article, 55% of *O Magazine* readers said Disney World was "the most terrifying place on Earth" for summer vacations. This external report only validated what we had started to see internally.

We had been successful in spite of ourselves for those past few years. Our attendance was at an all-time high, but our guest satisfaction scores were on an increasingly steady decline. And that's not unusual—historically, guests aren't as happy when it's crowded. But we're Disney, and we could do better. That article was the punch in the gut that ended up changing the trajectory of everything.

The Chairman agreed that yes, we would be investing into these new experiences as Meg had proposed. But we had to invest into improving the base experience as well. The directive was clear—the guest satisfaction issue had to be taken care of. The question was, how?

Following this meeting, Meg thought over the weekend about what the Chairman was asking them to do. The more she thought about it, the more she realized that because of the silos and lack of connectivity across various business units, this was an impossible task for his executive committee to accomplish in a "business as usual" environment. They all had too many individual responsibilities to come together and focus on this. From her perspective, the only way to make this work was to identify a key subset of direct reports, put them on a team, and create mutual accountability to get it done.

The Chairman agreed and chose a team of four from his executive committee to define exactly *what* needed to be done and the scope of work. These four included Meg herself, plus Al Weiss, Bruce Vaughn, and Jim Hunt. While leadership was definitely attuned to the end-to-end experience, this was the first time a team consciously took a step back to think holistically and inclusively about what was going on. This endeavor was given the working name of "The Next Generation Experience."

Together, they created a charter statement that outlined the problem—we had become a highly-dense, highly-attended destination resort, but we haven't really done anything to personalize our guests' experiences. Our skyrocketing attendance and growth had created a wonderful problem, but a problem nonetheless, where we were constantly in a peak period and had taken a mass anonymous approach to our business, which is the price tag of volume.

To fix it, we had to focus on the total guest experience and identify what had to be improved from a fundamental level. This would include a focus on lines, hassles, barriers, and friction points, along with striving for personalization and customization. Needless to say, there was a major task at hand.

With the *what* defined, they now had to figure out the *how*. The team of four formed an exploratory team of five to spend eight weeks peeling back the guest experience, identify all the friction points within it, and ideate some possible solutions. This team of five came from all aspects of the organization—Andy Schwalb in Technology, Eric Jacobson and Kevin Rice in Imagineering, John Padgett in Business Development, and myself in Operations. I'd also be remiss not to mention Dan Soto and the critical role he played in integrating all of our efforts, as well as Gary Daniels, who led a module-level team focus on My Disney Experience capabilities.

At the time I was approached to join the core team of NGE, I was admittedly a little reluctant to leave my day job for too long. We had some wind in our sails from the success of our 25th at Epcot and were running on all cylinders. It wasn't easy to go while things were going so well, so I initially agreed only with the stipulation that I'd remain the VP of Epcot until we knew the NGE boat would float.

But I am in no way trying to say I was hesitant about the opportunity whatsoever. I had vaguely heard about this new project going on and had a lot of curiosity about it, but I didn't think it would come my way. Joining the team and contributing to NGE are some of the proudest moments of my career, and I am honored to have been a part of it. While I kept one hand on the wheel back at Epcot and had a great team to keep things running smoothly, I jumped into the front lines of innovation.

Working out of a trailer at Epcot, we were a self-led group with no appointed head. It was a very different way of doing things, but then we were trying to do something very different—we were working to raise the baseline of our guest experience. And for the first time ever, we were given the go-ahead to evaluate the end-to-end experience with a hypercritical eye and propose radical solutions that would forever change how we did things as an organization. It was a lot to do, but we were given the support, tools, and time to do it.

We spent the next eight weeks traveling between Team Disney/Burbank and Disney World to understand the complete guest experience and identify every friction point we encountered along the way. Every point where we had to stop—parking, turnstiles, lines, and any other hassle—was meticulously noted and assessed.

From there, we created a roadmap of the guest's journey and divided it into five categories—pre-arrival, arrival on property, on-property experiences, departure, and the post-trip. The hope was that by the time they got home and reflected on their trip, they would think back on a great experience. Well, all of our data points told us they weren't having the best time like they should.

Even something as simple as booking through our vacation planning system was difficult—our website was archaic, cumbersome, and confusing. Okay, so that was Data Point #1. Main Street USA was no longer the entrance to Magic Kingdom where guests could meander down and become immersed in the experience—it'd become a thoroughfare highway for people to beat cheeks down and grab their FastPasses for the day. Data Point #2. You could check into The Grand Floridian for the 30th time, and the front desk would *still* ask if you'd been here before. Data Point #3. It went on and on.

From booking, traveling there, checking into our resorts, going to our gated attractions, traveling back home, and everything after, the process was bumpy and difficult. The process was also much too transactive and anonymous—we didn't know our guests, and it showed. By experiencing our parks like a guest, we were able to conclude that the current experience was not satisfactory.

Simply put, we needed to do better.

We decided that we needed to take a hard look in the mirror and created a paradigm shift in our thinking as an organization. There was a gap between what we were doing now—ignoring current consumer trends, offering episodic experiences, complex transactions, and an anonymous approach—and what we needed to do—embrace innovation, create immersive experiences, turn transactions into interactions, and personalize our approach for each guest.

So, we identified the problem. Now, how can we create solutions to make the guest experience more immersive and seamless? What and where can we connect things to transform the episodic and anonymous experience into an immersive and personalized one? How can we integrate advancing technology while still empowering our cast members to make the magic?

These questions drove us to finding the solutions that would move our complex and transactional current experience into a simple and seamless future one. We created pitch points of what we believed those solutions were, and we knew it wasn't going to be an easy fix.

We had to:

- Define our guiding principles to create forward momentum.
- Break down the silos between the parks, resorts, and other attractions to create a seamless experience.
- Empower our cast with the tools and resources to make their jobs easier.
- Establish an *experience foundation*.

Our proposed means of accomplishing these things were what became the:

- My Disney Experience
- Magic Band[4]
- FastPass+
- MyMagic+

Without question, it would take a lot of time and resources to do all this. We also weren't proposing that these were just one-time actions to fix the problem and never think about it again. Nope—we were proposing radical and permanent actions that would completely change our way of doing things. But if we could pull it off, we would raise the baseline guest experience to new heights and completely innovate

---

4 Funny story—the inspiration for this came when, while on a flight to California, John Padgett was flipping through Sky Magazine when he came upon a magnetic wristband that allegedly cured almost everything in life. He ripped the page out and said, "This is what we need to do!" And, that's what we did.

the landscape of our organization forever. We just had to get the executive committee to see that, too.

As our eight-week deadline approached, we knew we had to cobble our findings and proposals together into a top-notch presentation to convince them this was the right course of action and worth what would ultimately be a billion dollar investment into the project. One thing was clear—a PowerPoint wasn't going to cut it. We decided that the best way to talk about it was to *walk* them through it and let them experience the proposal for themselves.

We found some available real estate in a warehouse out by the Imagineering HQ in Glendale to create our "walk-through" presentation. When the Chairman and his executive committee arrived for a half-day presentation, we walked them around the many scenes and prototypes we created to demonstrate how our ideas would work through the guest's journey—what our website booking capability could be like, how the transportation from Orlando's airport to the check-in of our resorts could be like, how FastPasses could be booked, what the new turnstiles could look like, and on and on. And yes, we really did all this in eight weeks! It was admittedly impressive visuals, but it wasn't just for show—we also included some consumer insights and light evaluations to show the viability of actually doing this.

Our consumer insights were pretty great, by the way. The concept of replacing the many "Keys to the World"—the room cards, theme park tickets, FastPasses, etcetera that guests carried around—with one wristband had an overwhelmingly positive reception. Every guest we talked to loved the idea of a single-form factor to consolidate the currently disparate media filling up their pockets. Really, all signs pointed to yes.

"Game Day" came upon us rather quickly, and it was obvious that our presentation blew them away. I mean, we came back to them with the entire vacation experience flipped on its head and a clear articulation of high-level strategies for major improvements in such a short time frame. I don't think anyone was really expecting us to bring so much richness to this initial assignment. It goes to show that when you give people dedicated time and permission to attempt to do the impossible, it can indeed happen.

The Chairman was obviously impressed, but he and the executive committee also had a lot of questions. While we'd done a lot more than expected in eight weeks, it was pretty clear that there was a lot more to do. We were sent back on another 8-week assignment to do some further vetting of our ideas.

That was the best news we could have gotten. Instead of basically saying, "Nice ideas, let's put them on a shelf for another day," we were given the validation that we were onto something after all. I like to joke this was the eight-week assignment that turned into eight years, because that's how long this whole thing turned out to be.

Of course, we didn't know this at the time. All we knew was that we got approved for another eight weeks on it. We would report back, get assigned eight more weeks, and so on. At some point, we started to enter the Great Recession, which placed an enormous pressure on the entire financial ecosystem to downsize and cost-cut. Given this major external factor, we didn't even know if it'd be financially possible to implement this at the time.

It was a lot like playing fetch—they'd throw that stick out, we'd bring it back, and they'd throw it out again. The thing is, none of us ever really knew where that stick would land. We just continued to work as the 8 weeks turned to 16, 24, 32…

We went down this refinement route for about a year until we had a clear proof of concept and cost-benefit analysis, at which point we had to prepare to present it to the Board of Directors for the ultimate approval. No pressure.

We had to convince our senior leadership team that not only was this the best solution to our current experience, we also had to convince them to reframe how they evaluated the key question: *Will this make us money?* The answer was too complex to answer with a simple P&L. It required us to maintain our usual analytical rigor and, at the same time, be a lot more intuitive to understand how, in the long run, this would be well worth the investment. For me, this was my first clear understanding of the importance of balancing art and science.

As Wayne Gretsky said, "I skate to where the puck is going, not where it has been." We had to get it into the senior leadership's head that we needed to be forward-thinking and prospective about where the industry was going, rather than where the industry is. Personalization, customization, and widespread use of technology was rapidly growing, and we had to get ahead of these consumer trends.

We created another lab out of the now-defunct space inside Body Wars at Epcot. Each node of the guest's journey was built out further and our prototypes were further refined, while a tech team figured out how it would all work. We were all constantly testing and adjusting to further the concept enough to know it'd work. Eventually, we vetted it out enough and got our lab to the point where you could quite literally walk through the at-home planning, the arrival experience, and every other step of the experience.

We had some promising feedback. Bob Iger came down for a vacation with his family. When visiting Walt Disney World, he always dedicated a few days for business updates, which included walking through our lab. While our lab was admittedly still pretty primitive, Bob was engaged and had a lot of questions for us as well. At the end, he outright told us that this was what he was trying to do across the entire organization and he thought we were, I quote, "years ahead" of everyone else. Our CEO gave us the biggest pat on the back you could ever imagine—nothing could have been more validating that we were on the right track.

Alright, let's jump to February 18th, 2009. By this time, I'd been running Epcot and doing the NGE thing for about 15 months. My team at the park had been very gracious about the fact that much of my focus was elsewhere and I managed both responsibilities as best as possible, but you ultimately can't be in two places at once. That would all come to a head on this date.

So on that morning, I was running on the treadmill when I got a note from HR: "Every word that comes out of your mouth today needs to be clear and confident." Which, geez, way to ruin the whole treadmill moment, but I digress. I was called into a meeting with my boss's boss. In light of the major headcount reductions taking place due to the Great Recession, I was admittedly nervous as Hell about what could possibly be going on.

In this meeting, I found out I was moving out of Epcot—it was a great run, but in hindsight, it had to happen eventually—and moving full-time to lead the due diligence period for NGE to formally vet out the concept before we could take it to the BoD. In a tight time, the organization preemptively recognized enough value in NGE to dedicate resources and talent to it. That's big.

Our due diligence period lasted about eight months. During that time, we built a newly-refined, fully-modernized lab in Soundstage 3 at the Studios to eventually walk the BoD through, and continued to make progress on the concept with further testing and evaluation. It was also in this time that "IBFW" came around.

I was walking around with the then-CFO of Parks & Resorts and talking through some investment stuff independent of NGE. He had recently come back to the company, so at some point I started to explain everything that we were doing.

"This is all pretty complicated, isn't it?" He asked.

"It is complicated," I said, "but if we stay true to our basic principles, our brand, our experience, and as long as our cast loves and delivers It, and as long as our guests love and use it, and oh, by the way, IBFW—It Better Friggin Work. So, as long as we nail all of *that*, then all will be well."

And as we were nearing our D-Day to get the Board's approval, what else was there to say? IBFW came to be my legacy statement and the rally cry through the due diligence period. It better friggin work.

The Board came through[5] and toured our lab in the fall of 2009. All of our hard work paid off—they loved it. The Board authorized the NGE effort and all it would take to make it happen. In December of that year, they announced that we would be moving forward with the Next Generation Experience.

It was official—we were greenlit. Full steam ahead on radically evolving our entire guest experience.

IBFW.

---

5   Minus Steve Jobs, who was unfortunately too ill at this time.

Decade IV

NGE, now known as MyMagic+, became definite just before the new decade started. As a part of the go-forward structure, I was promoted to the Senior Vice President of Walt Disney World Parks *and* the operational element of NGE. My responsibilities also included Workforce Management, Animal Programs, Experience Optimization, and a handful of other areas. So, there was a lot going on, but it couldn't be more exciting. I was back in Operations at the height of innovation and strong momentum in delivering our base business.

We spent the next couple of years testing and refining each aspect of MyMagic+, and getting our organization ready for what we were set to implement. Cast members needed to understand that the incoming technology would empower them to make the magic, *not* to replace them. Beyond that, changes of this magnitude take time to acclimate to. From top to bottom, we all had to prepare for everything to come.

This was all further complicated by the fact that we had to implement these changes while also still running all day-to-day Operations. In essence, we were trying to change the tires of a moving bus, a tough task for any organization to accomplish.

The pressure was intense for everyone across all disciplines, especially for the technology team. We were trying to do something really big here, so some hurdles were not unexpected. It wasn't anything horrific enough to shut the whole effort down, but there were times where we were backed up against the wall and it sure felt like it. There's no question the componentry of NGE was indeed complicated, and weaving everything together in an end-to-end perspective was very challenging. But, we put our heads down and worked through it. One element adding to the complexity of everything was politics—there were many different agendas in need of servicing and, in hindsight, while I feel really great about how we integrated all of this into the organization, there were relationship and transparency issues at a very senior level that created significant headwinds we had to manage.

Implementing something like this on such a vast scale is complicated. You can't just throw it on like a light switch and assume that everything is going to be okay. That's just not how it works. Based on all of the issues we encountered, we revised our launch schedule to be much more thoughtful and methodical than what we had initially planned.

Instead of a full and immediate launch en masse, we decided to roll it out incrementally to work out the bugs and build it up to a bigger scale. We started this gradual rollout at WDW in 2013 with our first priority of stabilizing our technology infrastructure, followed by the MagicBand, MyDisneyExperience app/website performance, along with FastPass+, the pre-arrival stuff...and on and on. Once we got the technology working well enough at the mothership, we knew it could scale to our other sites.

Earlier in my career, I was fortunate to recognize that implementing something like this actually does take a village, and I was surrounded by incredible talent to engage and deliver on how we would operationalize everything. Natalie Sirianni, Scot Reynolds, Carrie Sandusky, Gina Cordero, and Sheri Torres were just a few of the key team members who would put together the detailed plans on organizational engagement and help drive awareness and ownership early in the life cycle. In particular, Deb Hart was masterful at galvanizing the organization and unifying hearts and minds to go climb this mountain. This couldn't be a surprise. Leaders on every level needed to understand it, own it, and lead it.

After working out the bugs in the initial launch and some changes in leadership that would address some of the issues mentioned earlier...IBFW...well, it *did* friggin work. Our cast members adjusted well to their new expectations and, once we got through the initial rollout challenges, our guests strongly embraced this new approach to vacation planning and fulfillment—redefining the experience itself.

The MagicBand in action.

Sharing the vision of the Next Generation Experience.

Honored to accept an innovation award from Fast Company for our NGE efforts.

Patents we received for our collective inventions during the course of NGE.

With that all said, I have a bit of a delicate point to make here. NGE was *never* a "project"—it was a transformation. And as a transformation, it doesn't have an endpoint. We had identified the dissatisfiers and implemented solutions, sure, but that didn't mean we were done. Not everyone understood that.

Too many people viewed the launch of MyMagic+ as the finish line. It wasn't. We now had access to real-time data and analytics to continue innovating the guest experience and Operations. That, to me, was only the starting line.

Regardless, the team was folded back into the organization shortly after the launch. While my position allowed me to continue to be a part of optimization and transformation efforts across the organization and I loved what I was doing, I wonder what more we could have done.

I mean, look at what we managed to accomplish when we were given the dedicated resources, license, and focus. It'd never been done before. Transformative innovation doesn't have a project closeout—you need to have a sustained focus to keep it going. And, based on organizational changes that had recently happened or were to come, nobody had any "extra capacity" to do more than what their day jobs called for. I firmly believe that aggressive and progressive change comes from incubation, and that incubation means organizations need to sign up for the right number and type of resources who will wake up everyday focused on these efforts 24/7. Admittedly, organizational tension surfaces when investing in efforts like this. But without this commitment, it will take on a "project persona" and vaporize quickly.

I want to pause here and switch gears to talk about an unexpected curveball thrown at me during this time. And that curveball was my diagnosis of prostate cancer.

Now, I hate when people say "everything happens for a reason"—I *know* the reason, but I sure as Hell didn't like it. I doubt anyone does. But I do believe everything that happens in life prepares you, in some way, for something that happens later on. In hindsight, this is a really good example of that.

My mother unfortunately passed away from cancer around the time we were opening Animal Kingdom, and although all of us had tried to spend as much time as we could with Mom, I wish I could have spent more...if just another hour, or even minute. So when my dad was diagnosed with kidney cancer at the age of 78 in 2011, I immediately made a commitment to become his caretaker and be as involved as possible—every doctor's appointment, every chemotherapy session, I was there. Those 18 months got me well acquainted with the journey I would soon face myself.

My dad passed away in November of 2012. My diagnosis came only a few months later. In a way, I was blessed with the sad but unique opportunity to learn so much about cancer before it literally fell into my lap.

In early 2013, a routine physical with my GP revealed that my PSA (which stands for Prostate Specific Antigen, a type of protein produced in the prostate) levels were starting to climb at an alarming rate. A high or rapidly increasing level is indicative of cancer. We had just buried my father and we were in the thick of the NGE rollout, so this news couldn't have been more unexpected.

Obviously, I very much wanted to eradicate this cancer from my body, and I visited a variety of doctors to gather as much information as I could to make the right decision for treatment. The best route was a prostatectomy via robotic surgery.

This surgery was a success, and my PSA started to drop. That didn't last long, though—soon after, it started to rise again. After seeking several medical opinions on how to address it, I chose to undergo radiation in town.

Once again, that was successful until, once again, the numbers went back up. On advice from my urologist, I got a C-11 Choline PET Scan, which was newly-approved by the FDA and could detect cancer on a granular level. For this exam, Marty and I traveled to the Mayo Clinic in Rochester, Minnesota, a place we'd become very familiar with in the next few years. We also met with Dr. Eugene Kwon, a world-renowned expert who actually drove the approval for the C-11 through the FDA. We were definitely in good hands here.

But much to our surprise, we learned the severity of my diagnosis was greater than previously understood. Based on that new information, we decided to begin drip-line chemo and hormone therapy immediately. Dr. Kwon's formal treatment plan was called "Intermittent Chemo and

Hormone Therapy," and after the first round, I was hoping the intermittent part would happen sooner rather than later!

Our routine for the next 18 weeks was pretty grueling—Marty and I would fly out to the Mayo Clinic on Tuesday night, I would have my drip-line chemo treatment on Wednesday, we'd fly back Wednesday night, and I'd prepare myself for the onslaught of side effects as I continued to work. Overall, it was tolerable, although there's no question that the fatigue and other effects came with a vengeance a day or two after treatments.

I need to say at this point that I couldn't be more grateful for the support from *all* of the folks in my world—my team, my leaders, my family, my doctors, everyone. While this was one of the greatest challenges I've faced, they all made sure I didn't face it alone. The company was also so gracious and ensured that my needs were accommodated while I could continue to be engaged in work, which I will always appreciate.

Fortunately, the chemo and hormone combo worked its magic, and my numbers became undetectable. This success continued for a couple more years until 2015 when, again, my numbers began to rise. Per Dr. Kwan's recommendation, I made the tough choice to do another round of radiation, this time at the Mayo Clinic.

I found a nice Airbnb within walking distance to the Mayo Clinic and moved to Rochester to complete a six-week round of chemo before undergoing radiation. These six weeks passed fairly quickly, largely because I got to work remotely during this. I initially planned to take a medical absence, but George Kalogridis, my leader and then-site president, knew me well enough to know I'd go stir-crazy if I did so. I was given the necessary accommodations to work to the capacity I could, which was an incredible thing that helped get me through treatment. Remote work access—which we all live and breathe now, but was quite rare at this point—was provided so I was able to maintain team connectivity throughout. Thank you team for putting up with that! I absolutely would have gone nuts if I wasn't able to stay connected with everyone back home. George even stopped in Rochester on one of his Orlando-California trips just to have dinner with me. These individual gestures and collective support of the company meant the absolute world to me.

This last round of treatments did the trick, at least for the next few years. While it wasn't the end of the road yet—and still isn't—I went back home and more or less got back to normal life. Aside from two substantial blips that I'll talk about later, my cancer has for the most part been controlled by the oral chemo and hormones that I take to this day.

The next few years saw major progress in the organization. All four of our theme parks had either recently completed or were about to embark upon major expansion efforts. The new Fantasyland opened up in the Magic Kingdom in 2012, culminating with the Seven Dwarfs Mine Train launch in 2014 which, coincidentally, was also the debut for NGE's FastPass+.

It was also during this time I started to work more closely with Josh D'Amaro, who had come in as VP of Animal Kingdom. We had actually met back in my Disneyland days, but we didn't work directly together. Even then, though, he had such a vibrancy in his leadership and was flagged early on as someone who was going places within the organization. Josh IS inspirational leadership. I could go on and on about what a rockstar he is...and a dear friend. Working together, we were a real dynamic duo.

Having been open since 1998, transformation efforts at Disney's Animal Kingdom involved a strong effort to position the park to be a full day and night experience. Pandora—The World of Avatar was the perfect anchor addition to accomplish that, however, the base park needed an uplift to support the additional capacity, which brought to life Kilimanjaro Safaris at night, numerous additions to the entertainment lineup throughout the day and night, and Rivers of Light (which deserves its own book).

Disney's Hollywood Studios began significant product transformation efforts, which involved reconfiguring the back third of the theme park to make way for Galaxy's Edge. This transformation also included new nighttime entertainment, Toy Story Land, and Mickey and Minnie's Runaway Railway.

The need to focus on revitalizing Epcot became top of mind for everyone. Epcot opened in 1982 and had been successful over the years, however, we all felt it was time to think about repositioning the experience around becoming more Disney, more family, more timeless, and more relevant.

Those efforts have been well underway for the last two years—minus a pandemic timeout—and will continue for the foreseeable future.

New attractions and entertainment experiences are always intended to be cutting-edge and highly immersive to bring guests directly *in* the story. And I can confidently say that over the years, with a handful of exceptions, we were able to deliver our legendary guest experience like never before. We truly unlocked the magic.

Alongside the explosive growth came significant reorganization within the company. High-level leaders were getting promoted, reassigned, moved between sites, and retiring. Change and developments of this caliber will inevitably create tension, so we definitely had some "growing pains" during this time. Different people had different ways of doing things, and it was a bit difficult for many to readjust.

Generally though, I'd categorize 2014-2018 as a period of intense concentration as leadership expectations were radically recalibrated from what had existed for the last two decades. We were pushed hard by our new chairman to take a stronger ownership position of our business, which included a much more direct focus on the commercial elements. On the surface, this may seem like an obvious expectation of all senior business leaders. However, there was a much different philosophy that had preceded these expectations. Along with George Kalogridis as the site president, Maribeth Bisienere, Thomas Mazloum, Josh D'Amaro, and I were resetting ourselves and the organization to these new expectations.

It was a very challenging time for virtually everyone. Really, it's probably safe to say that it was one of the best and worst times of our careers, but I'm excited to share that (almost) everyone passed this test and are stronger leaders as a result.

Additionally, there was intense pressure to redefine several aspects of the vacation experience with changes that would reorient several of our current offerings and take on a different look. A need for a more dedicated focus on the end-to-end experience was becoming more and more apparent to us. By end-to-end, I'm referring to the business rules and processes that stand across all of our businesses. While there were some differing opinions, it was obvious we needed a leader who could wake up everyday thinking about things holistically.

These thoughts led to the creation of a Chief Operating Officer role to focus on these gaps. As a result, I was promoted to what would be the final position of my career in 2018. This happened only after some resistance—from me. Based on my tenure and experience, I was working as the then-informal leader amongst the group of direct reports accountable to the president. Admittedly, at times, this was an exhausting load to carry. It was then strongly suggested by others that we needed someone to step in as a COO to run all of Operations at the WDW site. They suggested that someone should be me.

My initial reaction was one of caution. This caution was based on the fact that Walt Disney World, as the largest single site in the segment, was a massive beast, and it would take solid alignment and agreement on the details of what this role would encompass. Besides, I didn't think a site of this magnitude would really benefit from a COO role and it seemed too big of a role to take on without some significant process agreements and modifications beforehand.

After opposing it for some time, George called me to say, "I would really like you to think a little more about this COO thing. I think it has some merit." I'm always looking to consider other perspectives, so I was more than willing to keep my mind open to it.

"Let me think about it over the weekend," I said, "and I'll put some thoughts together."

I decided to do some serious soul-searching about this COO concept. I always have an innate desire to always understand the depth of purpose in these types of things. What was the purpose of this role? Why would we need one? I started by Googling the definition, and went down an illuminating path to learn what exactly a COO is.

Through my research, I found one article that I found particularly insightful from *Harvard Business Review* titled "Second in Command: The Misunderstood Role of the Chief Operating Officer." It gave seven definitions of a COO's function within an organization, as well as when an organization does and doesn't need one. One definition kind of matched what I was doing—as the glue that holds all of the various operations together to drive the business forward. That made a lot of sense to me.

After reading this article and reflecting on it, I realized we might need one after all. We were lacking the horizontal connection that a COO could create. They could connect the dots across the ecosystem and synthesize everyone's focus.

I could do that.

I called George back that Monday and told him I had reversed my position. Soon after, I was named up as COO in 2018. Ok, technically I was "Senior VP, Operations at Walt Disney World," a newly-created role. We almost never used C-suite titles for leadership at each site, but I was known internally as the COO of WDW. I refer to it as COO now because people immediately understand that role and the job description was the same. Regardless of semantics, I was responsible for Operations of *everything* at our site.

My first order of business was to look at synergies across everything at our site and make those points connect. By this time, Josh had left Walt Disney World to assume the role of the president for the Disneyland Resort, and Maribeth, Thomas, and I were driving Walt Disney World Operations. We had to get under a one-team mindset moving together toward a common purpose. This wasn't easy to do on a good day, much less amidst some of the ongoing political tensions within the company at the time. But with Thomas and Maribeth, we knew we could figure it all out and make it happen. I was fortunate to have been additionally blessed with strong thought and integration partners in Nancy Belanger, Kristen Barthel, Sheri Torres, Natalie Sirianni, and Ketan Sardeshmukh—extraordinarily talented leaders who knew how to thread our efforts horizontally across the broader organization. Later, I'll talk more about the importance of having leaders like these, along with Deb Hart and Sarah Riles, to help pave the way.

I was knocking on the door of 59. I took this job knowing it'd probably be my last at Disney. Especially for someone who started as a boat driver, it couldn't get any better than that, but sooner or later, I knew retirement would be inevitable and I'd have to launch into my next chapter in life. At this time, and even now, I was continuing with my cancer treatment, our teenagers were graduating from high school and going on to college, and Marty's consulting business was growing. I was coming to a place in my life where I wanted to spend more time as a husband and father, and therefore, the time was nearing for me to make a significant life change.

Beyond myself, this was also a period of immense change across the leadership landscape. In the spring of 2018, Catherine Powell was appointed the President of Parks West, which included Disneyland, Walt Disney World, and Disneyland Paris. Catherine brought an immediate and contagious level of realistic positivity and light to the culture, as well as a strong focus on the cast and the business. She quickly sensed that we all needed this infusion and, indeed, we greatly benefitted from her presence. In the summer of 2019, Catherine commissioned work on and a focus of the strategic side of business transformation. Sarah Riles—an absolute rockstar who deeply understands and leads with a cultural and business transformation mindset—

and I were tapped to lead these efforts for the site, with a strong connection to the segment transformation. This was a game-changing move to zero in on how to move the business forward. Unfortunately, this effort was cut short with Catherine's "sudden departure" in the fall which, given her strong influence across the organization and iconic presence as our leader, devastated many of us. We will ALL forever remember Catherine for her innate ability to Engage, Inspire, and Lead, and AirBnB is now very fortunate to have her at the helm.

In the fall of 2019, George was assigned the responsibility as the President of Segment Enrichment and the Ambassador for Walt Disney World's 50th Anniversary, a critical role in setting our sights on this important milestone. With George's new assignment, Josh moved back to Orlando to assume the role as site president.

At the same time, we were turning a corner in terms of positive momentum and performance. There was an element of excitement driven by a focus on our cast and taking our business to the next level. So I was juxtaposed between this renewed momentum on the work front and the personal desires mentioned earlier. I knew this was indeed going to be my last role and I would make the absolute best of it.

Our focus for the next several months was purely on alignment—creating a more cohesive and connected culture, eradicating any silos that remained, developing a set of standard processes and procedures across the site, and then staying in tune to all commercial and operational efforts to drive the business forward. We were all about new growth, but we were also all about injecting this energy back into the organization at all levels. Josh brought in a sense of renewed purpose with a focus on our cast and our guests. He's got a great mantra that I think exemplifies inspirational leadership to a T: "Bow, Rise, Stretch, and Fly." That is, BOW to our cast, RISE in our delivery of guest and cast experiences, STRETCH our thinking and expectations, and FLY on the winds of optimism and inclusion[6]. Optimism and positivity at the site was running high. We were doing really well.

It was the best job ever but, with great leaders steering in the right direction, I had to consider my contributions to the organization along with my health and longevity in the workforce. In early 2019, signs of my cancer returning had become evident. That March, I found myself back at the Mayo Clinic to treat a re-emergence of my cancer in its initial place of origin. This resulted in some pretty intensive surgery in my prostate bed to remove the cancer via cryoablation, where they basically freeze the cancer to kill it off—pretty high-tech stuff. Luckily, the surgery was successful and I returned to work shortly afterward.

While it was a bit of a wakeup call to evaluate my priorities, I didn't have much reason to retire in the immediate future. We had a lot of positive momentum, accomplishing our goals, making significant contributions, engaging and inspiring

---

6   This is a paraphrase from the full quote.

the cast at all levels, and delivering great results. Really, I was having too much fun to retire just yet.

Now, fast-forward to December of 2019...my cancer had returned. We discovered that I had another area of metastasis in my esophageal lymph nodes, which led to thoracic surgery in January of 2020. This surgery was a lot harder than the last. It was an extremely intense and extremely scary operation—the metastasis was in a tricky area between my esophagus, lung, heart, and aorta. Since it was so difficult and dangerous to access, they had to go in from several angles on each side of my chest to remove it. As invasive and complicated as it was, this surgery was thankfully a success as well.

It was a big lightbulb moment, too. I took a step back and thought about my longevity and my life beyond the workplace. After two aggressive surgeries in less than a year, I'd be a fool not to. These kinds of life-quaking events would make anyone reassess things.

2020 had quickly proven to be a much more challenging year for me. I admittedly had some distractions concerning my health when I returned to work in February. There was already a lot going on when *kablam*—COVID hits.

Alright, we all know what COVID is by now. And, unfortunately, we've *all* been affected by the pandemic in some way, shape, or form. At the time, we really didn't know what was going on or how long it would last. One thing, though, was clear—this was going to be a challenge unlike any other. Those of us on the site's steering committee, regardless of discipline, got serious fast—we created a special task force, set up a command center, and began to draw up plans in the case of a temporary closure. Deb Hart, Nancy Belanger, Sivonne Davis, and Darlene Papalini, along with the rest of our site's VPs, played critical roles in developing the planning and activation efforts.

Our planning and activation efforts were all-inclusive. It had to be—we knew every aspect of our organization was going to be affected. One morning in early March, we were feverishly working on our plans when we were paid a visit by Bob Iger, Bob Chapek, Zenia Mucha, and Jane Parker, who had all flown down from an event in New York to review our plans. The gravity of the situation was obvious, and little did we know that right around the corner, additional leadership changes were about to kick in[7].

Our thinking at the time was that we'd have to temporarily close within a week or two. By that evening, "within a few weeks" turned into "within a few *days*." All of the plans we had created for the possible future were accelerated to *right now*. We immediately announced our plans to close the entire resort and executed them on the night of March 15th, initially with the idea that it'd only be until the end of the month.

---

7 These included: George Kalogridis named the President of Segment Enrichment and Ambassador of the 50th Anniversary and Josh D'Amaro named as George's replacement as site president in November of 2019. In February of 2020, Bob Chapek was named to replace Bob Iger as CEO. In May of 2020, Josh was named as Chairman to replace Chapek and Jeff Vahle was named as his replacement as the WDW site president.

After we closed, many of our cast members were furloughed while the rest went effectively remote to continue our recalibrations. Only a "Ride-Out Crew" remained on site, a lean team who ensured our infrastructure was maintained and safe. All other agendas were cast aside while we focused on the dilemma. The health and safety of our cast members and guests were at the top of our minds. In all the uncertainty, we worked every minute of every day to steer our ship through the storm.

The complexity and magnitude of the decision to close really can't be understated. The size of the property and number of moving parts at the site is mind-boggling, and it took the entire weight of the site's leadership and steering committee to calculate exactly what a closure like this would entail.

We've closed plenty of times due to hurricanes and other natural events. Being in Florida, it comes with the territory. We are well-versed in handling crises and have an operating plan in place for just about every scenario you can think of. But this was a very different story. Nobody could have ever foreseen the complexities of this, and the swirl of rapidly-changing information made it difficult to anticipate what would happen next. With no clear light at the end of the tunnel, it was the most excruciating period of uncertainty that any of us had ever faced.

It was an immensely challenging time on a global, organizational, and personal level. As someone who'd just recovered from surgery and was considered extremely immunocompromised, I was worried. While we wouldn't yet understand the severity and impact of the pandemic, the MacPhee household locked down, masked up, and did everything we could to prevent the spread of the virus.

During this time in lockdown, I received a sign. I was setting up my home office when I found a little card in one of my notebooks. The card was from a sort of thought tree Marty sets up during Thanksgiving and Christmas. This one quote that I drew from the tree was one from Francis Bacon, which said this:

> *"Begin doing what you want to do now. We are not living in eternity. We have only this moment, sparkling like a star in our hand and melting like a snowflake..."*

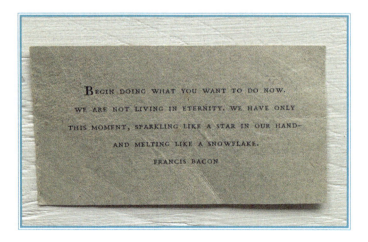

Talk about a sign! It practically screamed at me to start paying attention to myself and my health. I mean, why else would I have found *that* quote at *that* time? It brought a moment of extreme clarity and inspired me to make the formal decision to retire. I wasn't done yet, though. First, I had to complete my final mission at Walt Disney World—reopen the property.

The question was, when? And how? Planning for our reopening turned out to be much more challenging than planning for our closure, and we were not yet sure what the trigger points would be for it. Really, we were blind as to when we could even contemplate a reopening. Cast members were asking us questions that we just didn't have the answers to, and that was really hard. For what seemed like forever, we hunkered down and figured out what we were going to do.

As part of a company with both domestic and international reach, we had the benefit of benchmarking. Our Shanghai site had closed and reopened ahead of us, which established a precedent we could base our response on. We began convening with representatives from all of our sites to share thoughts, best practices, and overarching safety protocols for reopening.

Once we understood how we could do it safely, reopening became our #1 priority. The six weeks we spent creating and proposing our reopening plans was the most intense period in my entire career. I'm not exaggerating by any means—in an extremely volatile and high-stakes situation, we had to make the best decision we could with the information flying around our heads 24/7. That's as intense as you can get.

Everything we did, we did for the health and safety of our guests and cast. And we had to do *a lot*—limited capacity, temp checks, ground markers for social distancing, among many other logistics. We even went around the parks with measuring tapes to ensure everything was marked 6' apart down to the inch. Beyond that, I also worked to knit together the story arc to pitch the reopening to the local government, our cast members, and guests.

Storytelling is an immensely important part of leadership. Everything you do—as an organization, as a leader, as an individual—has a story. People respond to and connect with stories. You have to tell them the right one to get them on board with the direction you are trying to take. We'll go into more detail on this concept down the road, but the crux of it here was this—if we were going to reopen, we had to get the story right, and it had to be one that we believed in 100%.

While all of this was extremely complex, it became clear that we had to simplify it to the best of our abilities. We all agreed that our approach would focus on basic reopening guiding principles. Like our rollout of MyMagic+, the reopening would be done in a thoughtful and methodical manner, one in which we would launch, learn, and adjust along the way. We knew we wouldn't have 100% of the answers right away. But if we were at least 75% right, we knew we were headed in the right direction. Our mantra would always be "right before fast."

The pressure was on. All of our reopening plans were set and ready to be implemented. Disney Springs was already up and running—yay Matt and Roz!—so we had a live-action model to demonstrate our protocols before we conducted a detailed site tour with Orange county representatives to see their application in the parks.

In order to reopen, Mayor Demings, his staff, and the Economic Development Council needed to approve all of our protocols. I was set to pitch our plans to these constituents on May 26th. Needless to say, there was a lot riding on my 20-minute presentation. We were 24/7 in the preceding days preparing for this—with legal, public affairs, and others reviewing every word of the presentation.

On May 26th, I presented to the mayor and his economic advisory council he established to approve reopening plans throughout Central Florida. Rather than a live and in-person presentation, I did this from a broadcast in the conference room at Team Disney. I was sitting there with Adam, Ketan, and Nancy, on pins and needles the entire time leading up to it. Just before I went on, I looked at the screen and said, "That's such a sterile shot. Hold on a second..." I ran into my office, grabbed my statue of Mickey Mouse, and put him in the backdrop. A small detail, but that's all part of the storytelling too. And PS, it also got a fair amount of media airtime too.

After we had given our proposed reopening dates and protocols, it was pretty clear that we were going to get the go-ahead to reopen. That was the big hurdle to jump, and we'd done it. We started our reopening first on June 11th at the

Moments before presenting our reopening plans with Mickey.

Magic Kingdom and Animal Kingdom, with Hollywood Studios and Epcot following afterward on July 15th. In my nearly 43-year career, this was to be my last big act and finale in the organization. The only thing left to do was announce my retirement and prepare for my departure.

Discussing the reopening on Good Morning America.

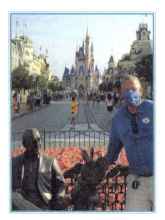

Reopening day at the Magic Kingdom on July 15th, 2020.

Now, remember that we had a major leadership change in the midst of all the closures and associated craziness. Bob Chapek moved from his role as the Chairman of Parks, Experiences, and Products to CEO of the Walt Disney Company. On May 18th, the new Chairman was finally announced—Josh, the current WDW president. Replacing him was Jeff Vahle, another fantastic leader and longtime great friend. As we adjusted to the many changes in the world and within our organization, I knew we were in good hands.

During my first breakfast meeting with Jeff, whom I had known and worked closely with for such a long and wonderful time, I shared with him confidentially that I would be retiring in the spring of 2021. I officially announced my intent to retire on December 16th, 2020 and served my last official day at Walt Disney World on April 1st, 2021. Yes, on April Fool's Day. And no, it wasn't some well-planned prank after all. I even made a presentation titled "Jim MacPhee's Retirement Plan" just for the occasion, which Jeff still ribs me about to this day.

As you can imagine, there is a lot of "hemming and hawing" when you make a decision as big as this. I've learned the validation of whether you've made the right decision happens both in the ten minutes after you first communicate it and then when you wake up the next day. Suffice to say, I knew I made the right decision.

When you announce your retirement, it's easy to fall into lame duck status pretty quickly. So while I made my intent to retire known many months before I actually did so, I made it clear that I would stay on only so long as I continued to add value and deliver excellence as I had before the announcement. Those final months were just as rich, productive, and fun as the rest of my career had been and on August 11th, 2021, I was honored alongside Phil Holmes, Trevor Larsen, and Djuan Rivers with a window on Main Street, USA.

The window on Main Street, USA. My name is the third one in the bottom left corner. (Image taken by Joe Burbank for the Orlando Sentinel.)

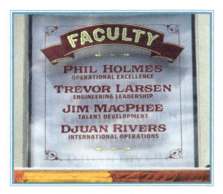
Closeup of the window. (Image taken by Joe Burbank for the Orlando Sentinel.)

Anna, Marty, Carter, and me in front of the window.

Awards I received to commemorate my 10th, 15th, 25th, 30th, 35th, and 40th service milestones with the Walt Disney Company.

I am so proud of what we've done and honored to have led so many incredible cast members. Like many things in life, there were ups and downs, but we were always working to do something amazing—bring the magic to life for thousands of guests every moment of every day. We all contributed in some way to deliver an experience that so many people will remember for a lifetime. My four decades with the company was a dream job through and through.

Like I've said, I try not to look back for too long, but I could not think more fondly of the time I spent at Disney and will always hold everyone I've worked with close to my heart. But now, I'm looking forward. Everyone in the MacPhee household has opened a new chapter of their lives—Marty and I have gotten into the consulting business, Anna and Carter are in college—and the future is bright. While I'm enjoying the extra beach time and traveling, and continuing to focus on my health and win my battle against cancer, I'm also exploring new and exciting ways to be a stronger force and make this world a better place on every dimension of life that I can. And I am *so* excited about everything I have ahead of me.

Anna and Carter on their 18th birthday at the Grand Contemporary.

Family time in Arizona.

Passing the legacy baton on as Anna MacPhee becomes a new cast member 5/24/22!

Now that you've stuck with me this far to understand my career and experiences, I'll tell you what I learned from it. Next up are the principles and beliefs that have come to define my leadership DNA and how they relate to "Engage, Inspire, Lead."

INTRODUCTION TO INSPIRATIONAL LEADERSHIP

Okay, it's time to get into the good stuff. Why can some leaders get their teams excited and dedicated to their purpose, and others struggle to do so authentically? How do you shift away from a compliance-based culture to one fueled by genuine commitment? What's the magic behind inspirational leadership?

The truth is, it isn't as complicated as some people make it out to be. It's actually very simple. It doesn't come from a manual, or a program, or a playbook. It comes from your heart and your mind.

Some people do say that leadership is magical, and that may be true, but it's not about *making* magic—it's about unleashing the magic already within ourselves. It's about mindfulness, about being present in the moment and not distracted by tasks, devices, the future, and other barriers to engagement. All that stuff can wait. Really, it's about putting those things to the side and focusing on the moment you're in, the people you're with, the here and now.

The key to success here is building authentic relationships with the people around. Engage them, inspire them, lead them. And that's really it.

When you commit to getting to know the individuals you work with on a deep, personal level, you're making an investment in them and yourself. This investment, of course, pays off—when you engage them in the purpose and inspire action toward that common goal, you can do *anything*. However, the commitment *has* to be real, it has to be genuine, and it has to demonstrate that you care about the people who are going to climb the many mountains ahead with you.

I believe this is the exact key that unlocked the magic throughout my 43 years at Disney. As Walt himself said, "You can design and create, and build the most wonderful place in the world. But it takes people to make it a reality." It's all about engaging the cast members who bring the Disney stories to life. Everyone at every level in any organization is critical to fulfilling its purpose and as a leader, it's on you to get them motivated and moving in the right direction.

An inspirational leader doesn't see their team as, say, 12 employees on whom they need to deploy various tactics to boost performance metrics each quarter; an inspirational leader sees their team as 12 individual people who they need to get to know, unite on the company's purpose, show how their role contributes to that purpose, and get them excited to work toward it with passion and commitment. In short, an inspirational leader recognizes that *relationships matter*!

I have come to understand just how true that statement is over years of life experience and, unfortunately, through loss. Nothing teaches you how important the people around you are than when someone is no longer here.

When I was in my early twenties, I witnessed my best friend, Steve, dive off a dock and break his neck after working

Grad Night together. I attempted CPR, but he didn't make it. Sharing the news of his death with his family was one of the hardest conversations I've ever had in my life.

As I've already shared, I lost both of my parents early to cancer and we lost our son three weeks after he was born, and that's had a permanent impact on my life. I realize I'm not alone in the experience of loss. While we will all experience a loss at some point, that in no way makes anyone's experience any less sad or significant. This stuff stays with you and reveals the fragility of life in a way you can't ever forget.

So, *carpe diem*—life is too short not to enjoy and be joyful about everything and everyone around you. To have a good life, you have to do what you like and like what you do. Otherwise, what are you even doing? My whole career has been about delivering results, but more importantly, having fun and creating an environment where everybody showed up and worked harder because they could be their authentic selves and part of a bigger purpose. For this, I have been very fortunate.

The point here is that if you want to be an inspirational leader, you have to recognize that relationships matter and build authentic connections with everyone around you. When you do this and do it right, you truly begin to lay the foundation of your legacy.

During the latter part of my career, I spent a lot of time seeking to understand what defines a successful and inspirational leader. And, in doing so, I created a series of principles, the baseline expectations every leader must meet to be successful, and beliefs, more esoteric concepts that are a step above that, to articulate performance expectations for leaders at all levels.

Now, having sat back in retirement and taken some time to think about things, these principles and beliefs have converged into Engage, Inspire, Lead. As you continue reading, you'll see how the principles and beliefs are deeply embedded within the following sections. For clarity and reference, here are the principles and beliefs listed below.

Principles	Beliefs
• Systems and Critical Thinking	• Connect to Your Purpose
• Mastery and Command	• Tap into Your Heritage and Tradition
• Effective Communication	• Lead with a Holistic Mindset
• RIKC (Relationships, Influence, Knowledge, and Credibility)	• Avoid Like-Minded Thinking...Find Your Contrarian
• Humility and Vulnerability	• Look Outside Yourself
• Trust	• Be Bold, Be Brave... Bravery Before Perfection
	• Lead with Clarity, Unity, and Agility
	• DiversiFY Everything!
	• Feed the Good Wolf

These have all fit nicely within the next three sections and served as the catalyst for the further philosophies and concepts we'll discuss. Boiling it all down to three simple verbs may make it seem easy, but as you'll see, there is a *lot* behind them. First, you have to engage before you can do anything else. That's where we'll start.

ENGAGE: RELATIONSHIPS MATTER!

Engage

"to hold the attention of: to induce participation"

"The harnessing of organization member's selves to their work roles; in engagement, people employ and express themselves physically, cognitively, and emotionally during role performances."

Introduction: Relationships Matter!

If you take only one thing away from this book, let it be this:

Relationships matter, and they matter more than you and I could ever really understand. At work, home, and anywhere else, how we connect and relate to those around us will dictate the successes—and failures—we realize in any of our endeavors.

I've always maintained that leadership matters, too. At Disney, the expectations on all of us, regardless of rank, are incredibly high. We especially ask our cast members to do the extraordinary and create magical moments that last a lifetime for our guests. With such great goals, it's our job as leaders to clearly define and communicate what needs to be done. We also need to model what we're asking them to do by doing it for them—if I'm not creating the best experiences for my cast members, how are they supposed to turn around and do it for our guests?

Performance, productivity, and fulfillment of an organization's purpose is ultimately driven by leadership at all levels. This is an important fact that cannot be forgotten. It's so important that when I was COO, I took it upon myself to start the #LeadershipMatters! campaign to showcase the amazing leaders in the field.

I'd go out to all kinds of areas around the property—Fort Wilderness Ranch, Toy Story Land, a breakroom in one of our resorts—and film a quick interview on my iPhone to get the word out on who these leaders were and the great things they were doing. It was informal, and that's how I liked it. I wanted to recognize these leaders, appreciate their hard work, and emphasize the importance of what they were doing. In short, I just wanted to show that leadership matters, and that didn't need to be put into a program.

"Programs" reek of a serious lack of authenticity. Authentic engagement is far more inspiring to me than anything else, especially during an extremely difficult time where internal pressures were at an all-time high. I knew I was spending too much time in admin areas and meetings, and not enough time where the magic really happens—on the front lines. So I took my phone, went into various operating areas, and connected with the cast members out there.

These organic, one-minute clips were met with a lot of wonderful feedback and infused so much positive energy into the organization. The impact of #LeadershipMatters! has been incredible, and I believe it's come to be a part of my legacy.

But as I've reflected back on the beginning of my career and this book, and where we are now, it's clear the relationships I've built with others have been the greatest part of my legacy and the catalyst for my successes. More importantly, these relationships are my greatest source of joy.

We all only have 24 hours in a day. If we roughly spend about 8 of those sleeping, 8 at play, and 8 at work—though it never turns out to be an even split like this—that means we spend about a third of our lives around the people we work with. Again, we spend *about a third of our lives* together running day-to-day operations and collaborating on the organization's forward destination. With that much time there, why wouldn't you want to at least get to know them?

In my very strong opinion, the act of engaging *authentically* is paramount. I'm not talking about the common transactional and episodic engagements many people do throughout the day. Asking how someone is doing as you pass by in the hall is not enough. Are you *really* asking how they're doing, or are you merely fulfilling a social obligation?

Transactional engagements lead to transactional leadership, where you just tell people what to do. But relational leadership and engagement is about getting into their hearts, knowing their backgrounds, understanding their challenges, learning their Why. The core of a successful relationship goes much deeper than these surface-level interactions, and they start to form on minute one of hour one of day one.

Disney's organization runs on a first-name basis. You can tell someone's name as well as their hometown just by looking at their name tag, which is a valuable tool for opening conversations between cast members and with guests. For leaders, this is a tool to get beyond cursory information and figure out what makes people tick. By approaching them sincerely, you can start to understand each individual's Why—why are they here, what motivates them, what do they hope to accomplish? This is the foundation of a successful relationship.

Engagement is a constant process, and nobody is doing it perfectly all of the time. At Epcot, our leadership offices were directly adjacent to the hallway into the Cast Services building. Every single cast member coming to and from their shift at Epcot walked through here. This was also where the restrooms were. When I'd head to the restrooms, I'd often be on my Blackberry (no, not the fruit...the actual device) as I walked. One day, it occurred to me that my Blackberry was acting as a barrier between me and cast members. Instead of engaging with others, I was focused on an electronic device. Talk about a missed opportunity! From that day forward, I did my best to look *everyone* in the eye and ask them how they were doing whenever I went through there. Like I said, asking is only the first step—listening to their response is really the key. These brief exchanges opened the door to engaging as many of our cast members as I could.

Speaking of doors, there was one in that same hallway with a big "Leadership Center" sign overhead. *And the door was always locked.* That irritated me to no end—here we were as leaders sitting in the Leadership Center, with a closed and locked door! I immediately went to find Sheri, my HR partner, and went for a stroll. I asked Sheri to indulge me in a brief pretend scenario—say we were new hires and we wanted to go see the leadership team, and came upon that locked door. How would that make us feel? What message did that convey about leadership and relationships here? After that day, that door was never locked again.

Because relationships do matter, and how we initiate and engage with others sets a precedent for everything we have and will become as leaders in an organization. At Disney, our success is dependent on the consumers' relationship with our brand, and our cast members are the enablers of that relationship. Who at the parks makes it a lifetime experience for guests? Are you going to think about the policies implemented by leadership of the company, or are you going to remember the fantastically eerie bellhop on the Tower of Terror who made the story come to life? It begins with me, and this act of building a relationship with the team—on every level—is critical to engaging and inspiring them to climb the many mountains with you.

You can first start connecting with others by removing your barriers to engagement. This can mean your phone, laptop, locked office door, tasks weighing on your mind, the things happening around you, anything that distracts you from the person right in front of you, right this moment. That person takes precedence over all of these things, no matter what.

Have you ever walked into a store—to pick up dry-cleaning, place a to-go order, check in for an appointment, etcetera—only for the person at the counter to take a phone call instead? How did that make you feel? Probably not great. You probably felt like you, the person physically standing there, were less important than the phone.

And when you take a call in front of someone, you are doing the exact same thing to them. By answering the phone, you are saying they are not your priority and you kill your ability to engage them. Now as a leader, you might think, *Well, I have to answer, it could be important!* Well, that person is important too. If it's not an emergency, let it ring. You can always call them back.

While I've certainly been guilty of this myself, I've worked hard to remove these barriers of engagement for myself and my teams. I've brought a basket into meetings for everyone to place their phones in. After all, our administrative assistants knew exactly where we were if there was an emergency. I would tell my own leaders that I prioritized whoever I was talking to in-person over any phone call, which led to a few scenarios: my leader would either agree not to call me during the day-to-day unless it was an emergency so I'd always pick up on those rare occasions, they'd call knowing I may not answer and would get back to them afterward, or, if they expected me to immediately pick up at any time, I'd preface each in-person conversation with that information so they wouldn't take it personally if I had to answer my leader's call.

When having these conversations, it's easy to default into talking about work right out the gate. However, before talking professionally, talk personally. Try to open a dialogue about who they are and what their life is like. Do keep in mind that some people are not receptive to this, and that obviously needs to be respected. But the whole point of engagement is to *connect* with the person, not the profession, so always resist the temptation to jump immediately into work.

So, next time you're walking down the hall or in the elevator, take the opportunity to engage with people you pass along the way. Look them directly in the eye, say hello, learn their names, ask how they're doing. But don't stop there. Get to the root of their motivations, their goals, and why they come to work everyday. This is the start of building a relationship and the foundation of inspirational leadership.

Key Takeaways

- **Relationships matter.** They are the catalyst to success, the legacy we leave behind, and a prerequisite to engaging your team and building commitment to moving mountains with you.

- **Transactional engagement does not build a relationship.** Saying a quick hello to someone is not how you get to know them, and neither is a conversation strictly about work.

- **Remove your barriers of engagement.** Distractions like devices and other internal worries keep you from being present and in the moment with those around you.

- **Understand who they are and what makes them tick.** Initiate conversations that help you learn who they are and why they are here. Knowing their goals, motivations, barriers, and enablers are how you can connect with and motivate them on a personal level.

RIKC

While building relationships with those around you is the foundation of inspirational leadership, it's only the very beginning. You can't reach your full potential unless you balance a strong focus on building relationships with the other aspects of leadership. That's where the RIKC Model comes in.

RIKC stands for Relationships, Influence, Knowledge, and Credibility. I developed this model shortly after being promoted to the VP of Park Operations Line of Business in 2004. I'd inherited a newly-formed organization that hadn't yet been able to make an impact from a leadership perspective. Upon some further digging, I realized that some within the team couldn't build those relationships because they weren't really "walking the walk," so to speak. They weren't working to develop or improve their knowledge, credibility, or influence on the broader organization. That's not a recipe for successful leadership.

As the leader, it was my responsibility to both model and hold leadership accountable to continuously investing in RIKC—building relationships, developing their influence, broadening their knowledge base, and establishing credibility. The RIKC Model, albeit informal, became the barometer I used on myself and others to ensure everyone was working on their self-development to further impact the organization.

Building relationships is only the first step. There's a difference between being *sociable* and engaging to make an impact. Relationships are the bricks to build your leadership and lay your legacy. You still need the tools and skills to do something meaningful with them.

While RIKC is something I always talked about and used to gauge how effective leaders were within their areas, there were no posters around the office or anything to make it official. It's also something I and some of the people close to me have been working for many years to fit neatly within the acronym, and we couldn't even get it to be spelt right! That was the hardest part. But the acronym shouldn't drive the philosophy, and it's really only used here to reference the idea that the knowledge you gain and the relationships you build will directly result in what influence and credibility you have in your organization. So, RK=IC. RIKC. You get the idea.

Again, relationships are only one immensely important aspect that we've already covered, so let's talk a bit about knowledge. When stepping into a new leadership role, some people may think that what they already know to have gotten there is all they need. That business degree or past experience is seemingly enough to inform what they're doing now. And if they've grown up in the organization, they may make the mistake of thinking they already know everything. This is simply not true.

Knowledge is your mastery and command of everything in your area, *and* understanding of the front lines. If you expect to lead these teams, you need to know what they're doing, how they fulfill the greater purpose, and what their challenges are. And you don't learn that by reading reports from the comfort of your desk—you need to get out there and see for yourself.

Whenever I had a new direct report as the leader of the parks, I'd tell them, "As you step into this role, I don't want you in Team Disney meetings or worrying about what's happening outside of this park. I want you spending every minute of your first 60 days out in the field. Get in costume, work with the third-shift custodial department, learn as much of the park Operations as you can."

Now, did I expect them to know the holding temperature of the walk-in freezers or how to launch a boat on the Na'vi River Journey? No, that wasn't the point. The point is to show that you're willing to learn what they do by doing it yourself and, as a result, even the playing field. By putting yourself on their level and walking in their shoes to understand how they step, they'll respect and step with you.

This is what I call RIKCing—getting on the front lines to build your knowledge base and develop relationships, establishing your credibility and strengthening your influence as a result. At the end of the day, RIKC really means that you can't just talk the talk; you have to walk the walk, too, or else you'll never become an effective leader. It all goes hand-in-hand.

Key Takeaways

- **RIKC stands for Relationships, Influence, Knowledge, and Credibility**. It's an informal way to measure how effective a leader is within their organization.

- **Walk the walk**. By getting on the front lines, you can gain in-depth knowledge on how the organization runs and develop relationships with your team.

- **RK=IC**. How much you invest into your relationships and knowledge base directly results in what influence and credibility you have in the organization.

Your Circle of Influence

Coming off of our discussion of RIKC, it makes the most sense to now introduce and discuss your Circle of Influence. Truly great leaders understand that their role is not one-dimensional. It's not just about inspiring and leading your teams—you have to consider your broader influence in the multiple spheres you encounter within an organization. The Circle of Influence depicts each relationship you have and need to maintain at every "level" in the organization.

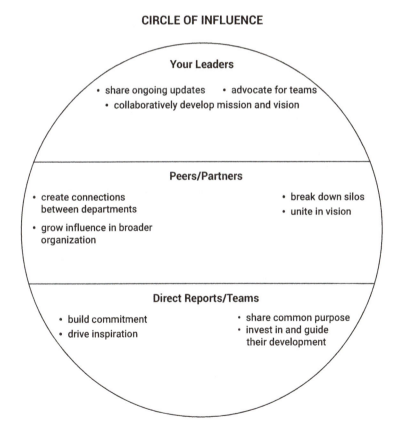

The first level is your relationship as a leader to your direct reports. This is where you are most clearly engaging, inspiring, and leading. Among your many responsibilities here, you have to bring people in on the vision, build commitment, and make your teams excited to work toward the organization's purpose. Beyond that, you have to involve yourself in their development and guide them to realize their individual potential to the fullest.

The second level is your peer-to-peer relationship with other leaders of the same "rank" within the organization. This relationship is often the most neglected. While many people may have respect for their peers and bump into them from time to time, they forget to put any effort into getting to know or staying in contact with those outside of their day-to-day. In a way, it's out of sight, out of mind—why should you invest in a relationship with someone you don't really work with?

Well, here's the thing: you *do* work with them, even if tangentially. Back to RIKC, building relationships with everyone is one of the ways that you can build credibility and increase your influence on the broader organization. If your roots run deep, but only right where you've been planted, then you have not successfully grown your influence and, as a result, are not an effective leader.

The other thing is that an existing relationship with your peers makes it much easier and much less awkward when the time inevitably comes to ask a favor. We all have that colleague who only reaches out when they need something.

Do you roll your eyes when they call? Probably. How likely are you to do something for them when they ask you to? Probably not as likely as you are when a friend does.

A purely transactional relationship leaves a sour taste in everyone's mouth. By putting in the time to build relationships with your peers and interact authentically with them now, you create the reciprocity necessary for them to be more than happy to help when needed, so long as you're returning the favor. Tending to your peer-to-peer relationships is an often overlooked, immensely important part of increasing your influence across the organization and gaining the social points for getting the occasional favor.

Peer-to-peer relationships also help break down the silos in an organization. As an organization, we should all be united toward a common vision, but it's hard to do so when we're all sectioned off into our respective departments and lines of business. By extending your relationships past your own area and connecting with your peers in another area, these silos can be broken down.

The third level is your relationship with *your* leaders and, for lack of a better term, "superiors." The influence you've built through relationships with your teams and peers will eventually reach these leaders, which is often how they get their first impression of you. Beyond that, it's on you to build the relationship in a way that benefits your peers and teams.

By beneficial, I don't mean the transactional method of buddying up to further your own career. However, you have to fulfill your responsibility as an advocate for your teams and for any projects/solutions that you and your peers have proposed. There is a careful balancing act that has to be managed here between representing these interests and building your relationship in an, as always, authentic way.

I'd be remiss not to state here that the leaders we work for have many responsibilities, one of which is to advocate for their team members both individually and collectively—just as we do for our team. It's important they are equipped with the truth on what's happening, and that often comes with a stronger focus on multiple levels...not just your 1:1 list of tactical items.

While title should not matter, the fact remains that a certain hierarchy or order of personnel within an organization exists. And as a leader, unless you own the whole company, your position is somewhere in the second level of the Circle of Influence. As a great leader, you can see the multiple spheres in which you operate and how they differ.

Another aspect of your Circle of Influence are the individuals you routinely connect with to help shape your own personal thinking, which also includes an element of contrarianism. In addition to your typical direct reports, there are those individuals who have some pretty special and extraordinary talents. Early on, I referred to this group as my "inner circle," but quickly changed it to Integration Partners, since when you have an inner circle, nobody really wants to be in the outer circle!

These Integration Partners don't just "drive work horizontally" and leave collateral damage along the way—they are multi disciplined in their job and generalists in their actions. Collaboratively, vulnerably, and with the overarching vision in mind, they RIKC, sometimes without even knowing it. This includes HR (Wende, Sheri, Kristen), Operations Planning and Integration (Deb, Sarah, Nancy, Natalie, Carrie), Admin Partners (Shari, Judy, Jennifer), and Communications. These people were instrumental in challenging my thinking, helping me form strategies and tactics, and looking outside myself. They really are my heroes.

The goal we are hoping to achieve here is to establish an ongoing connection between all levels and lines of business within an organization, and that takes RIKCing and knowing your Circle of Influence. By understanding the three main dynamics you need to manage, you can successfully build relationships with everyone in your organization.

Key Takeaways

- **The Circle of Influence depicts your relationships on three "levels."** This shows the different dynamics that you will have in an organization.

- **The first "level" is your leader-to-team relationship.** This includes all of your responsibilities as a leader.

- **The second "level" is your peer-to-peer relationships, which are often neglected.** It's important to have an ongoing relationship with your peer group beyond asking them for favors to break down the silos and establish a holistic and end-to-end team dynamic.

- **The third "level" is your relationship with leaders.** You have to balance advocating for your teams and peers while also building authentic relationships.

- **Great leaders recognize that their role is not one-dimensional.** By understanding the three levels and how they differ, they can build relationships with everyone in the organization.

DiversiFY Everything!

In this day and age, the focus on diversity, equity, and inclusion has never been more apparent and necessary—and rightfully so. While we've collectively made a lot of progress, I've noticed that these terms can sometimes seem like some sort of separate department, program, or manual. Too often, these concepts are viewed as tasks to be checked off on a to-do list rather than as a continuous effort toward a better world. They aren't items; they're actions.

Right around when I became SVP of the parks, the senior leaders convened in a half-day session to have a conversation on diversity and attempt to unpack unconscious biases. While this was led by an excellent facilitator from the Diversity Department, it was obvious that all of us—me included—were just going through the motions of dialogue. As I think back on it, I think we forgot to pack our bags with vulnerability and authenticity—some of us were just looking for some program book so we could pivot and pass it onto our teams instead of opening up to identify and recognize unconscious biases on an individual and organizational level.

Going deep on that subject created a level of vulnerability that some were uncomfortable with. But we got through it and became an even stronger team as a result. When confronting a topic as difficult as this, some discomfort is to be expected, but it was in that moment I realized talking about diversiTY was just, well....talking. Be it a program book, manual, or the like, diversity was just a noun. So, I made a personal commitment to stop talking and start doing. I had to turn that noun, diversiTY, into a verb and diversiFY myself and my leadership.

Going forward, I made a conscious effort to lead through action. When I walked into a conference room before meetings, I did my best to never take the same old spot next to the same old person and talk about the same old topics. Instead, I'd look for the person I knew the least, sit next to them, introduce myself, and try to get to know them.

During meetings, I paid keen attention to who did and didn't speak, and encouraged those who were more quiet to share their opinion. Level, title, and tenure didn't matter—*every* voice in the room deserves to be heard. This was how I differentiated the aforementioned action of diversifying from the discussed-to-death noun of "diversity," and it was the impetus for several other key principles that would formally surface further down the road.

Was I perfect all the time? Hell no! But, I was conscious of my behaviors and actions. People watch us constantly, and while these actions might seem small, the impact and impression they make on others is huge.

Each and every person brings a unique perspective and opinion to the table, and it's a leader's responsibility to create a supportive and encouraging environment where they are able to share them. Diversifying is ultimately how we grow and innovate—both as organizations and as individuals.

Several chapters—if not whole books—can and will be written on all we've learned about diversity, especially in the last few years. My main emphasis here is the action of diversiFYing, but I continue to be a student of diversity.

Key Takeaways

- **Live the verb, not just the noun.** We need to actively diversiFY rather than discuss diversiTY to truly be inclusive and progressive.

- **DiversiFYing starts with you.** Sit next to someone new and try to get to know them. Seek completely different perspectives. These small, constant efforts are how we can bring everyone to the table.

- **Encourage every voice.** Hearing everyone in the room is how we can see all perspectives and, ultimately, grow in the workplace and beyond.

Humility and Vulnerability

In the last section, we talked about how discussing diversity created vulnerability. And that's a good thing! Growth doesn't happen inside of your comfort zone. It's only once you take that first step outside of it that you can start to learn critical lessons and change for the better. Humility is one of the most important values a leader can possess, and vulnerability is a natural byproduct of that.

If you're looking for any recommended reading, one of my favorite books on leadership is *Good to Great* by Jim Collins. In this book, Collins identifies and describes seven key traits of organizations that can successfully transition to the upper echelon of success. My favorite was what he calls "Level 5 Leadership."

> "The most powerfully transformative executives possess a paradoxical mixture of personal humility and professional will. They are timid and ferocious. Shy and fearless. They are rare—and unstoppable."
>
> -Jim Collins,
> *Good to Great: Why Some Companies Make the Leap...and Others Don't*

From what I've seen, people define humility in many different ways. Some see it as a weakness they have to eliminate, while others understand it as a virtue that enhances who they are and how they go about the world. I, of course, subscribe to the latter. My family can attest to my passion for and commitment to having a sense of humility in every aspect of my life. While I believe humility has always been a part of who I am, I didn't quite realize just how important it is until the mid to latter part of my career.

Decades ago, I once dual-reported to two totally different leaders. They were polar opposites of each other in both experiences and values. One was driven yet grounded, a leader who thought all-inclusively and considered other perspectives. The other was self-centered, only focused on fueling their own ego and had no interest in developing any relationships beyond the one they had with themselves.

It was difficult to mitigate the contrast between the two, and I found myself going a bit nuts. I could not understand what exactly made them so different, and I also couldn't figure out WHY I was so conflicted about it. They were both recognized as good leaders, yet they were dissimilar in nearly every way. What made the disparity? I began to contemplate the values they displayed, and eventually realized what it was—humility. One had a sense of humility in everything they did...the other, not so much. *That* was the great difference between the two. Humility.

Up until this point, I had never really "studied" the concept of humility from a practical, biblical, or leadership perspective. I knew what it meant as it related to my own life and leadership, but I hadn't gone into any depth beyond how I had already come to understand it. When I get into a situation of confusion and conflict like this, I have to take some time to step back and reflect. Quite often, I'll start by Googling definitions to find the authentic definition of something and sort through the varied interpretations.

This is how I came upon various insightful resources, including revisiting Collins's book (and the Bible!), and formed the perspective I have today. And my take on it is this: Humility is a make-or-break factor for inspirational leadership. You can not authentically connect with others, consider differing opinions, and further your self-development if you do not live and lead with humility.

Authenticity is the prerequisite to inspirational leadership, and humility is the prerequisite to authenticity. How are you supposed to relate to others on a person-to-person level if you aren't willing to be yourself? Projecting some persona of what you think a leader should be won't do you any good. Vulnerability can be scary, there's no denying that. In some people's minds, to be open is to leave yourself open to potential threats.

At the end of the day, people connect with *you*. Not a facade, not a title, YOU. As Dr. Brené Brown said in her book *Daring Greatly*, "To feel is to be vulnerable." By having humility and allowing yourself to be vulnerable, you can then engage, inspire, and lead. It can't happen otherwise.

So, what does humility look like in action? Well, you can start by understanding your role and purpose within the ecosystem of your organization. I don't really mean your title—in fact, when I began to lead the parks, I sat down with everyone and asked them to pull out their business cards and read them to me, just as I did with mine. At the end of that, I declared that all of our business cards were incorrect. They talked about what we do, technically, but in reality, our roles were really that of an Experience Steward. That was my mindset in every senior leadership position I took on. When you know without question what purpose you serve within the organization, you neutralize hierarchy and remove any ego, real or perceived, from it.

As a leader, it's not just your "job" to engage and inspire others to fulfill their purpose to the fullest extent possible—it's *your purpose*. You can't do this from your desk; you've got to get your butt out of the office and onto the front lines. Actively and attentively listen to each person's needs, barriers, enablers, and goals—and use what you've learned to motivate them on an individual level.

Humility means you are willing to admit that you, as a human, are fallible. If you make a mistake, own up to it. If you fail, identify what went wrong and take responsibility. And when you don't shift the blame on others, you're able to learn and grow from each stumble along the way. That is the gift of humility.

As a leader, you must illuminate greatness. A leader without humility will choose to shine the spotlight on themselves; a leader with humility will shine it on others. Praising yourself only serves your own ego, but praising others shows them that their efforts are appreciated and positively encourages them to continue. Which one is more valuable?

The difference between a leader who creates inspiration and a leader who gives instruction is the ability to authentically engage with the people around them, which means stepping out of any "big boss" persona we may put on and connecting with each individual on the personal level. You can't do this if you aren't willing to open yourself up to others and be vulnerable. The openness to feel and allow others to see your true self—the essence of humility—is, in my opinion, also the essence of leadership excellence. While it's not the entirety, humility is ultimately a key ingredient in the recipe for great leadership.

Key Takeaways

- **Humility is essential for excellence in leadership.** You cannot authentically engage with others and become a truly great leader without displaying a sense of humility.

- **Vulnerability is a natural byproduct of humility.** While being vulnerable can be scary, it has to happen to genuinely open up to others.

- **Humility has many gifts.** By acknowledging when you are wrong and not having an ego, you can learn and grow from your mistakes when others would not.

- **Your title doesn't matter.** It's your role, how you contribute toward your organization's purpose, that does.

- **Showcase the greatness in others.** By drawing attention to members of your team and not to yourself, you can recognize the work others are doing and encourage progress to the next level of performance.

Trust

That word, "trust," is by definition pretty simple: "belief that someone or something is reliable, good, honest, effective, etc." But in reality, the meaning is actually a lot more complex. While there exist plenty of books and studies on the concept, sometimes someone will trust or distrust something solely because they "feel" that they should or shouldn't. There's sometimes seemingly no rhyme or rhythm to it.

In all of our lives, the notion of trust is omnipresent in just about everything we do. We make purchasing decisions based on whether or not we trust the product, brand, or company. We choose our friends and partners based on whether we trust them.

And our success as leaders depends on how—and how much—our team trusts us. It's either the wind in your sail or the anchor dragging your boat to a halt. Trust, or lack thereof, is what makes your team follow you to the ends of the earth or abandon ship. Trust is a major component of building commitment versus compliance and becoming an inspirational leader. When they trust you, they are happy to work hard and run in the direction you point toward. Really, you can't even be a good person—much less a good leader—without earning the trust of those in your life.

It's important to break down the various dimensions of trust so that when the perception of mistrust is present, we can understand *why* it's there—whether it's in your mind, your team, your leadership, or in the rest of the organization that you may interact with.

My favorite analysis on trust comes from field research conducted by Patrick J. Sweeney, a military psychologist and US Army Colonel who served in Iraq. Trust could not be more important and more apparent than in military operations. That's quite literally a life-or-death situation. Sweeney conducted real-time research on soldiers engaged in actual combat, so I'd say his findings have a lot of weight.

His conclusions broke trust down into what he calls "The 3 Cs": Competence, Character, and Care. What I love so much about Sweeney's analysis is that it gives solid components to an otherwise esoteric concept. I've personally used these 3 Cs to give feedback and assess direct reports who need to build more trust, and I've found that dimensionalizing it like this is both a much more effective way to give criticism and more well-received.

Imagine if your leader walked up to you and said, "I don't trust you." That'd be devastating, right? And you wouldn't even know *why* you aren't trusted. It feels like a personal attack that doesn't result in any improvement, so everyone loses.

Now, imagine if your leader walked up to you and said, "You're exceedingly competent in your position and clearly have a good character, but I think you need to engage with your team more. I'm sure you care about them, but you need to demonstrate that to them so they can trust you better."

While it's clearly a critique, it doesn't come off as an unproductive onslaught. There's no perceived insult, the gap in trust is identified, and what needs to be done to bridge it is clearly communicated. This is why I love The 3 Cs so much.

So, Competence, Character, and Care. These traits are ultimately what gets soldiers to trust their leaders in battle. Let's go through each and discuss what it looks like in the workplace.

Competence is pretty self-explanatory—do you know what you're talking about? Do you have the mastery and command to lead with credibility? In my opinion, competency not only means you are thoroughly knowledgeable and capable of your own responsibilities as a leader, but you are thoroughly knowledgeable and capable of the task you are asking them to do, too. You understand how their role fits into the bigger picture and can clearly communicate it. This is Competence with a capital C.

Okay, onto character. When a leader has high character, they espouse their organization's values at all times and act in a consistently "good" way. Honesty, integrity, loyalty, etcetera, are all the basic principles that someone should practice in life regardless—I'd hope that we all want to be morally upright people. At work and beyond, character is a huge factor of whether or not we trust an individual. If someone is true to their word and never strays from their convictions, we trust them. And if someone is known to lie or speculate without all of the facts necessary to provide an informed opinion, we don't trust them. It's that simple.

If someone asks you a question that you don't have an answer to, it's okay to say you don't know. More than okay, it's *necessary* to admit when you don't know something. I remember when Josh first met with the steering committee shortly after he came in as President of WDW. During that meeting, he made one of his key tenants *very* clear—be comfortable with the vulnerability of this statement: "I don't know." Nobody is expecting you to know everything at all times, and the only way to establish credibility and build trust is to be honest when you don't know something, but are willing to admit it and find out the answer.

We all know people who, when posed a question they can't answer, will make something up on the fly. And it's *so* obvious when they do. While some people become masters at improvisational lying, everyone around them will eventually catch on. One way or another, they get found out, and it totally wrecks their credibility. People will judge them to have a bad character *and* question their competency. It's a trust-breaking double-whammy.

On the other hand, when you're transparent about what you do and don't know, people tend to trust you that much more. This also goes back to humility—you have to have a sense of humility to admit when you don't have the answer, but are willing to work with everyone to find it. Saying "I don't know" can often be one of the best ways to showcase a high character and build trust as a leader.

One thing to note here is that character is not the only key to building trust as a leader. There's a big difference between trusting someone as a *person* and trusting that person to do their job. For example, say you have a friend who you know, love, and trust as a good person, but is terrible with time management and can't even calculate the tip on a restaurant bill. Would you recommend them for a high-pressure job at a bank? The answer, unless you secretly hate your friend, is no. While character is a key to trust, trust is not automatically bestowed based on character. You can have a good character, but if you clearly lack the expertise and practical abilities, your team can't trust you to lead them.

The last C, Care, refers to caring not just about your organization's purpose, but for your team who fulfills it. This goes back to authentic engagement and even to vulnerability. Remember, a leader is there for their team, not the other way around. At Disney, my job was to inspire and support our cast members on the front lines making the magic. Those who are most directly fulfilling your organization's purpose are ultimately the most important. Their success—or failure—is your responsibility.

For them to trust your leadership, they need to know that you care about them and are invested in their individual development and success. A caring leader demonstrates empathy to their team, understands who they are and what they do, and is clearly "with" them in everyday challenges. Engaging with your team, when it's done right, will show that you care about them. If your team sees that you are looking out for their best interests, they'll be willing to follow your lead anywhere.

Together, The Three Cs build trust between you and your team. Again, this is an all-inclusive effort. You can't *just* be exceedingly competent, or have high character, or care deeply for your team; the answer to building trust is all of the above. And you need to have all three, all of the time. Trust can take years to build, but only a second to break. Once trust is broken, it is very difficult, sometimes impossible, to recover from. As Lady Gaga once said, "Trust is like a mirror. You can fix it if it's broken, but still see the crack in th[eir]...reflection."

Trust is one of the most crucial elements of leadership excellence. Like humility, this principle is what separates inspirational leaders from the rest.

Key Takeaways

- **Trust has various definitions.** Why we trust something/someone and to what degree depends on various, sometimes arbitrary, factors.

- **Patrick J. Sweeney broke it down into The 3 Cs.** This analysis dimensionalizes an otherwise esoteric concept in a way that makes it easy to understand trust in the workplace and critique those with a gap.

- **The 3 Cs are Competence, Character, and Care.** Competence refers to your ability to do your job, Character refers to your morality/integrity/etc., and Care refers to your perceived investment into your team.

- **For trust to be built, a leader must display all of The 3 Cs.** One can't happen without the other, and they have to be consistent.

- **Trust is necessary for effective leadership.** If your team doesn't trust you, you're not getting them anywhere.

Look Outside Yourself

When innovating, dealing with a problem or making a tough decision, you might hear a common piece of advice: "Look inside yourself, and you will find the answer." For many, deep introspection is seemingly the best way to go. And while self-reflection is important, it's not the singular direction one should look toward—looking *outside* yourself is critical for getting new ideas, balancing your view, and keeping any ego in check.

This is something I wish I could've learned and practiced much earlier in my career than I did. However, it's never too late to understand that the power of an organization is the sum of *all* its people and those beyond, not just the smartest one in the room.

The collective expertise and experience at a company like Disney is extremely powerful. When you put that many heads together, it's almost impossible to encounter a challenge that hasn't already been faced in some way, shape, or form before. As a result, a long-established organization like ours is the best at solving a crisis and moving mountains. There's no question about that.

But when you've been the best for so long, you can get comfortable and set in your ways. You're looking inward because you like what you see, and that will come to keep you from advancing, optimizing, and transforming your business. The universal kiss of death for anyone at the top of their game is to assume they're always going to stay there. This is why you need to have the humility to seek other opinions and expertise.

Luckily, you most likely already have a cadre of incredibly sharp and talented people within your organization who are hungry to make a contribution to the growth in a really big way. It would be downright foolish not to leverage that resource, but there are surprisingly many leaders who do exactly that—they don't take advantage of the talent they're surrounded by, and then pay for it down the road.

One of my favorite concepts in looking outside yourself is the notion of Hunt vs Farm, coined by author Jeremy Gutsche. Many leaders are more than happy to stay on the farm, grow the same crops, and reap the same harvest over and over again because they know and are comfortable with the same old soil. After all, why fix what isn't broken? But an organization can only do the same thing for so long before it loses its energy and stamina. If you're not constantly working toward innovation, the status quo will stop working for you and you'll be left scrambling for a new plan. So before that happens, you need to go out and hunt for the latest and greatest to bring into your own organization.

Of course, this takes time and commitment, and in many cases, it's very difficult to do as an extension of your day job. As I've said before, smart organizations dedicate resources specifically challenged with this hunt for innovation. While they still need to be in touch with day-to-day Operations, hunting is a full-time job and needs to be treated as such because it is *that* important. Hunting for excellence is how you innovate, and recycling your success is how you can die as a business.

I've realized that the more I grew at Disney, the further away I got from the truth of what's really happening on the front lines. That's the unintended consequence of leadership growth. But, you don't have to let it keep you out of touch. To look outside yourself means to put aside your title and tenure, surround yourself with the most diverse group of thinkers you can find, and encourage—in fact, *insist*—they voice their thoughts and ideas with as much conviction as you do your own. Fostering and receiving a range of opinions from others is how you stay in tune and continue to develop your own perspective instead of falling stagnant.

When we were in the ideation process for NGE, it was not lost on us that each individual component of everything we were trying to do was probably already being done by someone, somewhere, somehow, in some way. That's inevitable. Simultaneous invention—where two people independently come up with the exact same idea—happens all of the time. But we had the unique ability to thread it all together for the end-to-end experience. That was our x-factor.

With this in mind, our approach to development intentionally relied on people outside of our organization and forced us to keep our minds open to new ideas. Even if our initial reactions were "We've already tried that," we wouldn't let that keep us from trying again, provided it made sense to give it another shot. The NGE team was notably diverse—we each came to the table with our individual expertise, but we respected and welcomed others outside of our respective areas to challenge our thinking at every turn. This is how we made innovation.

You might be the absolute expert of your area. You might know the business like the back of your hand and have been in the industry for decades. You might *not* see what value that someone on your team fresh out of school could possibly bring. What do they know that you don't already?

Here's the thing—*you do not know everything*. Beyond that, you are not omnipresent and therefore, you don't automatically see all perspectives. Each person in your organization offers new knowledge and a fresh perspective that you will not get if you don't actively seek it out. You need to create an environment where your team is not only comfortable to voice their own opinions, but actively challenge your own.

If you're in tune with what's going on in your meeting or a discussion, you can recognize who has something on their mind, but hasn't yet said it. It is incumbent on you to identify when that is happening and pull it out of them—not in a call-them-on-the-carpet kind of way, of course, but in a warm invitation out of respect for what they bring to the table. Showing that you appreciate and embrace these thoughts is how you will be able to solicit those amazing ideas that completely differ from your own.

Really, you need to find your contrarian, that one person who thinks completely differently than you do. They'll challenge your every idea and offer a polar opposite perspective for you to consider. This is how you avoid like-minded thinking, one of the perils of a mature organization.

When you have a room full of highly experienced and talented leaders, you will likely hear an echo chamber of opinions. Great minds think alike, this is often true, but just because everyone is saying the same thing doesn't necessarily mean it's the best thing for the business. This is also true in the rest of life. A differing opinion can help evolve an idea and ensure it's the correct course.

Some of the most powerful and rewarding things I have gotten to do in my life have stemmed from colleagues and friends who had the courage to challenge the status quo and disagree. Contrarians provide unexpected blessings if you let them. Being open to and accepting of divergent perspectives can sometimes be challenging to wrestle with—after all, we all think we know what's best. That said, you will quickly find the value of this broader level of thinking.

Jeff Vahle, one of my best friends and an extraordinary leader who today serves as the President of Walt Disney World, became my contrarian many years ago on both a personal and professional level. Whenever I was feeling really good about the direction I was headed, I would always go to Jeff to solicit his opinion and check my thinking. His views provided me with a wider array of thoughts that I could compare my own against and see how it holds up, which would either help me evolve my idea or strengthen my position on it. Ultimately, my contrarian gave me more options to move forward with, and that is everything in a high-stakes decision.

It's often challenging to find your contrarian in an organization with a lot of hierarchy. Let's be honest, we've all sat in an ideation meeting where the only "idea" is parroted from the most senior leader there. We've all also heard someone more senior than us say something that didn't resonate…or was just subpar. If contrarians are not encouraged, these ideas will go unchallenged.

Great leaders have the courage to offer their differing opinion, regardless of who's in the room, and create an environment where alternative ways of thinking are supported. And the greatest leaders listen first, assess the range of opinions, and lay out all the options for consideration… and are nimble and agile, open and honest with themselves and others too.

One of my favorite quotes comes from the Bible, Romans 12:2. "Do not *conform* to the patterns of this world, but be *transformed* by the renewing of your mind…" Conformity is the enemy of excellence. Sticking to the status quo will only hold your culture and business back from progress and innovation. Your expertise and experience should not be set in stone—new knowledge is constantly being acquired and views are constantly evolving. It's up to you to decide to participate in this change, and to reap the benefits from it.

Be a student of not just your own industry, but the world at large. Seek to understand the various tools and resources in place...outside yourself. Open your mind and get off of the farm where you've been tilling the same soil. Look outside, find your contrarian, and hunt for the excellence to adapt to your pursuit of transformation in your business, life, and mind.

Key Takeaways

- **Look outside yourself.** Seeking opinions and perspectives outside of your own is key to innovation and growth as both an individual and an organization.
- **Get off of the farm and go hunt.** When you get too comfortable doing the same thing, you won't seek new excellence until what you're doing no longer works.
- **Avoid like-minded thinking.** While the senior leader may set the pace of a meeting and the room may become an echo chamber, seek out and encourage different perspectives and opinions.
- **Find your contrarian.** Someone with completely different thinking can offer you a broader look and provide invaluable perspectives to consider.
- **Create an environment that encourages differing opinions.** Hearing everyone in the room is how we innovate and grow.

Be Bold, Be Brave

Ask yourself this: "What path do I normally choose in life, bravery or perfection?" Is it better to courageously advance into new and unknown territory, or to hold back until you are 100% sure of your journey and destination? The answer depends on the context. If you bravely decide to hike Mount Everest by yourself without any supplies, you're probably not coming back. And if you wait to ask out your high school crush until you know exactly what you'll say, you probably never will. In business, the path we should take has changed over time.

Historically, we've valued perfection. Companies used to focus on precision, on conducting exhaustive analysis of anything they're looking to pursue and completing everything to the nth degree before finally moving forward. That's how business used to be conducted, and that's what worked for a very long time.

But that doesn't work anymore. Waiting for perfection takes entirely too much time in the modern age. Our rapidly-evolving world moves so quickly that by the time an organization has achieved perfection and is ready to execute, the moment has already long passed.

Now, it's about bravery—that is, responsible and calculated bravery, not blind bravery. I believe any leader in this day and age likely has a very, very good sense of what their organization should be doing. If they think something is going to work and it's executed well, chances are it actually will work. These assumptions should always be softly validated by early analysis and research, but intuition should be trusted enough that this validation does not delay implementation. Companies that wait to make their decisions until perfection is achieved are only going to lose.

We are all smart people who've been doing this for a long time to get to where we are now. It would be fair to say we have a pretty good idea of what we need to do and how we need to do it to take our organizations to the next level of performance. If we did not, then we shouldn't be leaders. We need to trust our guts and listen to the intuition we've developed over the years and not fall into the trap of perfection. When industries move so fast, bravery is the only way to make progress.

It's not about having a 100% perfect score to move forward. It's about being 75% right and having the bravery to close the gap along the way. But you have to get the momentum going, and be nimble and agile as you go.

This concept of bravery over perfection really came through when Marty showed me a TED Talk of Reshma Saujani, the author of *Brave, Not Perfect*. She advocates for parents to encourage their daughters to be brave rather than perfect, and how teaching them to be perfect is only holding them back. As a parent, this was a very powerful lesson, and the shift from valuing perfection in women to bravery is fortunately starting to happen in the broader world.

You can even see it in Disney movies. I mean, "brave" is quite literally the name of a movie. Characters like Moana, Meredith, and Mirabel are far from perfect, but they have the courage to rise up against their challenges anyway—whether it's the Mother Island goddess, a bear, or a faltering encanto. These young women are brave, and that's what matters.

To value bravery means to embrace failure. Not everything you do is going to work. In fact, a lot of what you do is going to result in some amount of failure. *Nothing* is perfect and *everything* can be improved. That's just a fact of life. If you choose bravery, you are really saying, "I know this might not work out. I know this could lead to failure, but that's okay. I'll get up, see what went wrong, learn from it, and move on." This is the right mindset to have.

The fear of failure holds many of us back from achieving greatness. Most of the time, greatness can't happen without some failure along the way. Those who are brave see failure not as a devastation, but as a unique lesson they won't forget. After all, most people try not to make the same mistake twice.

So, we boldly strive forward, and we embrace the prospect of failing along the way. As a leader in an organization, bravery is what really matters. These days, perfection only impedes progress. So be bold, be brave...and perfection will follow.

Key Takeaways

- **In business, it's better to brave than to be perfect.** It's only recently shifted, and perfection used to be valued greater.

- **The world moves to fast to wait for perfection.** By the time the research and analysis is complete, the moment for execution has already passed.

- **Bravery means going forward without being 100% ready.** It's about being 75% of the way there and recognizing openly that while you still have more to do, you'll tap into the broader organization to bring it on home.

- **To be brave, you have to embrace failure.** Understand that failing is an opportunity to learn and grow, not a major setback.

- **Be bold, be brave.** When you decide to move forward, you will eventually create perfection along the way.

Summary

- Relationships matter, and authentic engagement is a prerequisite to inspirational leadership.

- RIKCing means to get out in the field to broaden your knowledge base and develop relationships with those on the front line, which directly results in your influence and credibility in the organization.

- DiversiTY is just a discussion. You need to actively diversiFY yourself and your organization to truly make an effort toward inclusion and equality.

- To connect with those around you, you need to have a sense of humility in everything you do. Vulnerability is a natural byproduct of humility, and you must learn to be comfortable with that.

- You must build trust to effectively lead. Trust can be broken down into The 3 Cs—Competence, Character, and Care—which has to be done altogether and all of the time.

- Looking outside yourself means to get off the farm, avoid like-minded thinking, and find your contrarian. Seeking out other perspectives, thoughts, opinions, and ideas is the only way to innovate and grow.

INSPIRE: TRANSFORM HEARTS AND MINDS

Inspire

"to exert an animating, enlivening, or exalting influence on"

Introduction: Transform Hearts and Minds

If you will briefly indulge me in an exercise, I'd like you to close this book, step back, and think about all the people who have inspired you throughout your life. Who were they? It might have been a parent, a teacher, a long-dead philosopher, a leader at your church, even someone on social media. Whoever they were and whatever it was, they brought you in on their message and made you feel as though you were a part of their journey. This is the outcome of inspiration.

Now, *how* did they do it? Likely in many different ways. However, every path to inspiration starts the same; everyone who has ever inspired you first engaged you in some way, shape, or form. There's no point in talking about inspiration without talking about engagement beforehand. You have to walk before you run, and you can't inspire someone before engaging them.

Really, this is all one big ecosystem of behaviors and emotions that collectively form the essence of great leadership. This is also exactly why it can be so challenging to unpack what the word "inspire" really means. I suspect we all understand what it means on the surface, but the core meaning and motivation can be a mystery. Who inspires whom? How? And the obvious question, why?

At this point, it's probably unsurprising to know that I delved into some deep research to get a better understanding of what it means to inspire someone. And wow—there are a *lot* of different takes on this. There were simply too many varying interpretations to list out and discuss here, but one theme was clear—awareness.

One of the keys to inspirational leadership is awareness. You must have awareness of yourself and others...on a deep, sometimes uncomfortable level. Everyone has the potential to be an inspirational leader. For some, it comes naturally. For others, it's a learned skill that takes time and study to acquire. Either way, it doesn't "just happen" as some incidental, episodic thing. You have to lay the building blocks of engagement first. Inspiration isn't a task you can check off your to-do list; inspiration is a daily effort driven by a higher purpose. It's an intentional, constant effort.

It's also impossible to inspire others until you've inspired yourself, and that takes deep introspection that some people find, well, not very fun. But you need to find and understand your "why"—what is your purpose, why do you do what you do, what gets you out of bed in the morning? What is it about your job that excites you each and every day? This greater purpose serves as your inspiration, and that's ultimately what gets you to inspire others.

Recall back to everyone who's ever inspired you. Specifically, think about inspirational leaders you've encountered throughout your life and career. Now think about those you found *un*inspiring. When you take inventory of what each did and didn't do, the contrast paints a compelling picture. For me, what those who have inspired me did was pretty clear:

- **Engaged everyone.** They invested in getting to know me on a personal level and understanding why I was there. In fact, they did that with most everyone.
- **Created a dynamic, exciting, and fun environment.** They included us in on the overall vision, and recognized and appreciated our efforts toward it.
- **Articulated a strong and compelling vision.** They were definitely focused on what I call "delivering the base," or the day-to-day tasks that had to be executed, but they also connected these efforts to our higher purpose. The destination was defined, and we were excited to get there.
- **Tolerated failure.** They understood that bravery is going to entail some errors along the way, and quickly addressed and forgave mistakes that were made. These blunders were then transformed into learning opportunities rather than catalysts for punishment.
- **Led with transparency.** They provided honest and direct feedback in real time. This initially may have hurt to hear, but in hindsight I ended up being a lot happier to know where I stood right then rather than later on.

These are only a few of the traits an inspirational leader can have. Looking back, it's easy to see how I took what I saw from them and adopted it into my own leadership mindset—and how all the better I was for it. In this section, we'll be discussing what I believe are the tenants for inspiration.

Key Takeaways

- **Engagement is the foundation of inspiration.** You cannot inspire someone if you have not engaged them first.

- **Inspiration is an intentional and constant act.** It doesn't happen by accident. You have to actively and continuously commit yourself to action.

- **Before you can inspire others, you have to inspire yourself.** Find out what your "why" is, and use that passion to ignite others.

- **Inspiration is the outcome of engagement, but there are various tenants of inspirational leadership.** This is what we'll discuss in this section.

Make Work Fun

If you crack open the dictionary and look up "work," you may find this:

"to exert oneself physically or mentally...in sustained effort for a purpose under compulsion or necessity"

Now I don't know about you, but when I read that, I was inspired beyond belief. *Not!* The sterile definition of work is nothing that would ever compel anyone to ever actually do it. And yet, aside from a nearly nonexistent percentage of the world, we all still work. The question is, why?

You're probably rolling your eyes and thinking the obvious, and you are correct—a paycheck is a primary reason. Most people work because they need income. The simple truth of the economy and job market is that money is a major motivator, and nobody can deny that.

But there are people who do not *need* to work, and they still do. Retirees who take a part-time job at their favorite store aren't really doing it for the discount, and neither is a socialite secretly running a charity doing it for the clout. When they aren't doing it for the money, they're doing it for personal fulfillment.

Whether it's to make a living or to make life better, I would say the work we choose is not based entirely on the paycheck. Theoretically, a sales assistant in a department store could make the same as a server in a restaurant. So why isn't everyone working at one versus the other? The wages are a big factor, sure, but it's the environment, energy, and element within a job that brings people in and gets them to stay.

People aren't working for just the paycheck. More and more, people want to know how their work feeds into a grander purpose. They want their jobs to have meaning, not just be a means of income.

Of course, your job isn't your life, but it is a third of it. And while most of us need to work to keep the lights on, we might as well make it fun. After all, life is too short not to have fun wherever you can.

Before we get into anything, I would be remiss not to remind everyone that there is a time and place for fun, and that is not *all* of the time. A meeting to determine layoffs is not fun, and it would be massively inappropriate to try to do otherwise. And we do not put other priorities to the wayside to be fun. It's about making our work, generally speaking, fun, without sacrificing focus on why we're all here.

At Disney, the bar is set pretty high. We're asking our cast members to do no less than make magical memories for our guests, but we all have fun doing it. I've noticed that the fun's been there since my days back in Watercraft. I had fun when we were busting our asses to open each park, in the thick of NGE, and every other transformative effort I've been a part of or led. When I had cancer, work was an important escape, not a burden. Why was work fun for me, and how did I try to make work fun for my teams? Let's explore.

As I've stepped back and thought about this, I've seen that the concept of making work fun is broken down into three aspects—the physical environment, the emotional environment, and the recognition and appreciation a team receives.

The physical environment is pretty obvious. It's hard to have fun in an office filled with cubicles and harsh overhead lights. What surrounds you day in and day out does affect you. If you're in a drab and dreary environment, it's going to take a toll. Any investment into this can be well worth it.

It can be small touches. At Animal Kingdom, we'd open each meeting with the Swahili greeting, "Jambo!" It's little things like this that can ground people to the organization and make the work fun.

The emotional environment is trickier to articulate. It starts by recognizing that people are more than what their business card says, but it goes far beyond that. Remember, engagement is a continuous process, and it's about routine acts of engagement to implement each day. There are daily things you can do to connect with everyone on your team and make the emotional environment flourish.

For example, I never immediately started a meeting with the tasks at hand. I wanted to hear about how people were doing, their families, all of that. We'd get to the agenda, of course, but it was not the immediate discussion. Instead of asking the group to go around and say something about whatever the topic was, I'd ask them, "Can you share a story about this?" That lifted us from the work to personal platform, created a level of vulnerability, and engaged the team.

Recognition and appreciation are two different, but important, things a leader must do. We all understand recognition. It's, "You did this thing, good job." You get a pizza party, a bonus, whatever, for a goal the team achieved or a milestone that was reached. When a team crosses a defined line and is given some sort of reward in return, that's recognition. As a leader, recognizing a job well done is incredibly important to team morale.

But *appreciating* an individual for what they bring each and every day—versus just a slab of pizza—is as important, if not even more so. Appreciation looks like this: you see what someone on your team does, and you sit them down and say, "I see you. I appreciate your hard work, honesty, intelligence, and passion. Our team is so much better with you here." Recognition is acknowledging that the team has done something, while appreciation is acknowledging what the individual contributes. A good leader does both, and understands when to do it.

Together, these three things are what I've seen culminate in a fun work environment. Engagement creates the dynamic and chemistry for fun, but there is one key element needed to make the mix—you have to share the purpose, too. If they understand why their work contributes to the ultimate purpose, they are going to be excited and have fun with what they are doing.

So, how do you make work fun? It's a little bit of everything—engagement, environment, and the right kind of meaningful praise. When people like where they work, feel their leader cares about them, and their work is valued, they have fun. And when people are having fun, they're enjoying themselves and contributing even more than they would otherwise. Making work fun is worth it, from a leadership and business perspective.

I'm a fan of quotes, especially ones that are simplistic in nature. One of my favorites is found on apparel from the Life is Good brand: "Do what you like and like what you do." To make work fun, I'd take it one step further: "Do what you like and like what you do...and like who you're doing it with." If we spend a third of our lives in the workplace, there's no reason why we can't enjoy what we're doing and the people we're doing it with.

Key Takeaways

- **Making work fun is about the physical environment, emotional environment, and appreciation and recognition.** These three things culminate in a fun work environment.

- **Recognition is acknowledging a team achieving a goal, appreciation is recognizing an individual's contributions.** Recognition is a collective praise, while appreciation is specifically for an individual. The two things aren't mutually exclusive, and the magic happens when you do both.

- **People have fun if they know what they're working for.** Include them in the purpose and tell them how their job contributes toward it.

- **When we have fun, we work harder.** If our efforts are recognized and feed into a greater vision, we enjoy ourselves and contribute more because we know we've played an important role in making it all come to life.

Connect to Your Purpose

Now more than ever, the world is wildly complex. Regardless of where you listen, you will hear a million different people saying a million different things every single day. Everyone is trying to pull you down their own route, and sometimes it can feel like you are getting torn apart in opposite directions. When a good leader comes in and leads people down a clear path that they are inspired to travel, they will follow them to the ends of the Earth and do the impossible. That is the great privilege of inspirational leadership.

But with that privilege comes responsibility, and one of the biggest responsibilities a leader has is to define and communicate the purpose in everything they do. Remember, people aren't *just* working for the paycheck. They want to know their job matters beyond the functions they perform. By clearly articulating the vision with conviction and excitement, your team will see it for themselves and be one step closer to inspiration.

Before they can be connected with and inspired by the organization's purpose, you have to do so for yourself. You have to understand *why* your organization does what it does and find the inspiration in it to then instill that in others. It all starts with you.

Hopefully, one of your own leaders has communicated the organization's purpose to you at some point. If not, then you may need to find or even define it for yourself. To do that,

I'll introduce Simon Sinek's Golden Circle, a concept that brilliantly explains the core of any organization.

In his book, *Start with Why*, Sinek describes the three layers of any organization's operation: What, How, and Why. On the surface, an organization's What is the most basic description of what service they provide or product they sell. At WDW, our What would probably be: "A resort destination with theme parks, attractions, stores, restaurants, etcetera." But as we all know, this is only cursory, and it's really so much more than that.

That's why we move into our How, or the specific things done to result in our What. Our How would probably be: "Bringing stories within the Disney brand to life in both real and fantastical experiences." That is the action we are doing, and the WDW property is the outcome of that. The How is more particular and deeper than the What, and most organizations won't have the same How. But now, it's time to cut deep into the Why—the incredible and unique reason the organization exists in the first place.

The Why is the ultimate purpose of an organization. At WDW, why do we do what we do? Why did Walt and his team turn a 27,000-acre plot of land in the middle of nowhere into a world-class vacation destination, and why do tens of thousands of people show up to work there every day? Simple—*to make magical memories that last a lifetime… for our guests and the cast we lead.* Everything we do, from selling Mickey pretzels out of food carts to building some of the most complex and advanced attractions in the world, is all to reach this ultimate goal.

With our Why defined, it's easy to see how each thing builds into the other: "We make magical memories that last a lifetime for our guests by bringing Disney stories to life in real and fantastical experiences at our theme parks, attractions, stores, restaurants, and everything else at our resort destination." By articulating the interconnected nature of everything in a clear and concise way, it's easy for everyone to see how every action in the organization ties back to the purpose. That is how you create inspiration.

Your organization's purpose, WHY you are all doing what you do, isn't (or, at least, shouldn't be) about money. A purpose is big, even lofty, something that will take the entirety of the organization to achieve. The numbers—gross revenue, quarterly reports, P&L statements, etcetera—aren't what get most people out of bed in the morning. It's the purpose that does, and it's the source and driver of continuous inspiration in the hands of a good leader.

Once you understand and articulate the entire purpose, you can then clearly communicate it to someone else and connect them to the purpose. At Disney, this starts on Day 1. One of my favorite things was the Heritage and Traditions class we took in orientation, which is still in place today. I remember calling my parents after my first day and telling them, "I don't know what exactly I'm going to be doing, but I know what I'm responsible for." Each individual job in an organization feeds into the larger purpose in some way, shape, or form, so everyone should be included in on the greater vision and shown how they contribute to it. This is how you can create inspiration at every level.

As important as it is to connect yourself and others to the organization's purpose, you also have to connect to your *life's* purpose. Remember, your job is not the entirety of your life. What do you do with the other two-thirds of your time? Great people always define the destination of where they're going in all areas of their life, and the purpose of the job they choose will often align with that of their life. The Why of their work is usually a spoke on the wheel of their life's Why. This, in my opinion, is one of the best ways to create balance among your previously-discussed four circles (remember: for me, that's Faith, Family, Social, *and* Career) and find a job most suited to you.

Setting your life's purpose is necessary to have fulfillment at the end of your career and beyond, and it's an incredibly personal thing to do. I mean, how would you respond if somebody just walked up to you and asked, "What are you doing with your life?" That's not my place here, but do understand you need to decide that for yourself sooner or later.

So, you can inspire others by connecting them to the organization's purpose. To do that, you first have to understand and connect to it yourself in order to properly communicate it to others. And beyond that, you also have to understand and connect to your life purpose, too. This is a major key to inspirational leadership and fulfillment. We're all here for something, after all. Show people how they're here for more than just a paycheck, and they'll be happy to show up and work even harder.

Key Takeaways

- **It's the leader's job to connect everyone to the purpose.** This is both a great responsibility and privilege.
- **First, you have to understand and connect to the purpose.** You can't effectively communicate the purpose unless you know it yourself.
- **An organization's purpose can be discovered by analyzing it through Simon Sinek's Golden Circle.** You can get to the core of your organization by determining its What (product sold or service performed), How (the actions specifically taken to result in the What), and then the Why (this is the entire reason behind the How and What).
- **Communicate the purpose and show how people at every level contribute.** Describe how the tasks they perform feed into the greater purpose.
- **You also need to define your own purpose.** For fulfillment, you have to discover the Why of your life, too.

Storytelling

Storytelling is one of the lesser-known arts of inspirational leadership. Whether I knew it then or not, I've come to realize the leaders who've impacted me the most were incredibly adept at telling stories. Crafting a narrative for your audience, situation, and objectives is one of the most effective and inspirational methods of communication. The main distinction between giving instructions and inspiring action is the ability to tell a story.

Now, by "telling a story," I don't mean telling a fairytale. When we're talking about storytelling, we're talking about telling a true one. Storytelling is all about how you tailor a nonfiction narrative, supported by your authenticity and credibility, to best appeal to and inspire who you're telling it to.

You might be thinking, *How is this relevant to leadership?* If so, you might be surprised to know that storytelling is relevant not just to leadership, but every single aspect of life. Since the dawn of time, humans have been telling each other stories. We have been hard-wired to listen to a story. That's what we connect with more than anything.

Humans respond best to a message that communicates to the parts of their brain controlling emotions, behaviors, and decision-making. A story does that. And when we hear a well-crafted one we can understand and relate to the most, we are willing to follow with our hearts *and* minds. A story, when done right, is how you can create inspiration in a big way and build commitment.

Storytelling is the heart and soul of what we do at Disney. Consumers of the brand see that in our films, shows, attractions, experiences, everything. But storytelling is also just as prominent behind the scenes. Every new innovation, expansion, and creation has a story woven inside and out.

Think about NGE. Do you think anybody would have been excited, committed, or inspired if we just announced, "We've noticed that our guest satisfaction has dropped, so we are implementing new technology in the park to improve the base experience." No! A sterile explanation is going to receive an equally unenthusiastic response. Nobody is inspired by that, not even the ones who said it. Now, compare that to the story that told the full depth of what we were doing:

"Our organization has been rooted in innovation from the start. Walt was a forward-thinker who not only overcame adversity, but used them as opportunities for advancement. When he lost the rights to Oswald the Lucky Rabbit, he ended up creating the Mickey Mouse we know and love today. Walt focused on relentless improvement and constantly redefined The Walt Disney Company, even when others couldn't fathom it. From cartoons to animations, to feature-length animated films to live-action productions, and all the way to the parks, Walt never stopped to look back. With five-plus decades of constantly looking forward, he left a legacy of innovation that we are picking up again with NGE. Together, this journey will help reduce our guest's friction points, utilize technology to create touch and turn transactions into interactions, and redefine the Disney experience itself."

Put yourself in a cast member's shoes and tell me which one would get you excited, inspired, and on board with the rollout. The answer should be obvious. This is how you bring people in on the vision and get them committed to its execution.

Now, there are three types of stories you will tell in leadership: one to inspire your teams working toward a goal, one to paint a picture of a problem to be solved with your partners and peers, and one to succinctly describe the situation to your own leaders. As each has a different objective, they each have their own separate guidelines to consider.

When crafting a story for your teams, you first have to consider how the agenda at hand ties back your organization's purpose. Great leaders express the Why before tactical statements. Not every task will necessarily need a story, though. It is more than enough to say, "Hey, please move this trash can about ten feet back so it doesn't block the parade." That's an episodic act that a cast member doesn't need to connect with and commit to.

Now, think about the cast member charged with sweeping up after a parade on Main Street. This is an essential and continuous responsibility, and they need to know the full story behind it. While there are many effective approaches to telling this story, there are some definitively right and wrong ways to do this.

"Hey, go sweep up Main Street." *Giving an order is simply not enough here. The cast member is not given the bigger picture and doesn't see how the constant task they've been charged with contributes to the purpose.*

"As you know, Show is one of our Five Keys[8] and a major part of the experience, and cleanliness is a really, really important aspect of Show. So when you're out there with a pan and broom after the parade, you're not just sweeping, you're re-establishing the environment conditions for Show. By delivering on this Key, we're ultimately able to all deliver the experience our guests have traveled for." *By describing the entire depth of the situation, the cast member is included in the bigger picture and can see exactly how they play a role in it.*

As you can see, a story tailored to your teams has to include the Why at some point and tie back to what they are doing. Beyond that, you need to understand the basic elements of a story that you need to include in your own. But we don't need to become creative writers here. These are

---

[8] Again, the Five Keys are Safety, Courtesy, Inclusion, Show, and Efficiency.

the fundamentals that you need to know as they relate to storytelling in inspirational leadership.

- **The protagonist.** This is the main character or hero of the story. The protagonist here should be defined collectively as "we"—uniting your audience with yourself and the rest of the organization.

- **The conflict, goal, or desire.** This could be a minor task to be done immediately, a large project to undertake, a barrier to fulfilling the purpose to be removed, etcetera. It is the main "point" of the story you are telling to inspire your audience to action.

- **The resolution.** This is the proposed outcome that should happen upon completion of the above point. Your audience should understand that this resolution does indeed make a difference and will be motivated to make it a reality by the end of your story.

- **The theme.** The organization's purpose. Your story always has to include the Why and connect back to the grander vision.

Much of what we've just discussed is also applicable in storytelling to your partners and peers, however, the goal is a bit different. Since you are at the same "level," for lack of a better term, your objective is not necessarily to inspire them toward action in their specific role, but rather to describe a problem to solve together or to present your solution in a way that convinces them it's the best way to go. With this in mind, it's pretty easy to recalibrate these aforementioned story elements to fit that objective.

When your audience is your own leaders, it's a totally different story. You don't need to connect them to the organization's purpose, and you don't necessarily need to inspire them. At best, that could come off as a condescending waste of time. Storytelling for your leaders means describing the current situation or problem and what's being done or the proposed solution, without leaving anything out.

The objective here is to paint the full picture of what's going on. I can't tell you how many times I received an inadequate email that only led to more questions. If it takes a lengthy back-and-forth exchange to get the full story, you didn't tell it right. By thinking end-to-end and having the necessary knowledge base of your position, you can craft a story that will avoid this headache.

First, consider whether what you need to communicate is most appropriate via a text, phone call, email, or in-person conversation. When in doubt, go for the "longer" one. I've gotten too many texts that should have been a phone call and emails that should've been a conversation. The method of delivery can sometimes be just as important as the actual message itself.

As a general rule, I don't like to engage in deeper, philosophical issues in any other way than a live conversation, be it in person or over the phone. Being able to hear the emotion of the individual I'm speaking with in real time is important. One tactic I identified early on is to "breadcrumb" my leader or partners on a deeper, more philosophical thought for them to think about before we actually have the conversation to go deeper. But I always caveat that by calling it for what it is—a breadcrumb to stimulate thought for a more effective, live conversation. Again, *how* you communicate it is just as important as *what* you are actually saying.

The key here is to tell the story in its entirety. Some might think it's a waste of time to include supposedly "unnecessary" information, but it's actually a waste of time *not* to, since they'll have to ask for it anyways. By frontloading the story with everything they need to know to understand the whole situation at a macro level and then providing the details behind that, you will communicate way more effectively than if you only first tell them what you think is most important. The whole story will generally consist of the points below.

- **The punchline.** Unlike a typical story, you need to get to the point right at the beginning.
- **The background.** You need to provide the contextual information so that what's currently going on will make sense.
- **The current situation.** An explanation of what is presently the issue or happening.
- **The complication.** Describe what has happened that caused the topic to surface and necessitated attention.
- **The proposed/ongoing solution, if applicable.** If something needs to be fixed, include what is being done or what you believe should be done with a holistic mindset.

When following these points, you will be able to tell the whole story as efficiently as possible. I know this can be difficult to picture, so I'm including a few examples below. Let's say a popular attraction has broken down and is temporarily not operational. Here is a summary of an email I actually got that didn't tell me the story from end-to-end:

Ride's down. We have welders on site to fix the problem. The work will last from second to third shift. Hoping to reopen tomorrow morning. I've notified everyone else.

Now, that email only created more questions. Why is the ride down? What happened? How are they going to fix it? If the full story had been told, that email would have looked more or less like this.

A situation occurred around 6 pm on the attraction and we are going to be down for the rest of the night, hoping to reopen with the park tomorrow. Somewhere around the third scene, a guest's leather jacket fell out of the ride vehicle and onto the track, bounding up the rotational gears of the vehicle. Since the vehicle was unable to rotate, it essentially caused the vehicle to jump the track and bend the towbar and track while ripping up some of the floor as well. We have welders onsite to [full description of the work here], which last from the second to third shift. Hoping to be back in operation by the park's opening tomorrow. I've notified [specific names/departments].

It's a little lengthier, sure, but it fully and completely describes the situation and what is being done. Anyone reading this would have few, if any, questions as a result. Storytelling for your leaders simply means telling the full story.

Whether we know it or not, we tell and hear stories all day long. That's what humans do. As a leader, you're already doing it, even if unintentionally. By consciously and thoughtfully crafting narratives for each audience, you can inspire your teams, find solutions with your peers, and communicate effectively to your leaders.

Key Takeaways

- **Storytelling is human instinct.** We do it every day, whether we know it or not.
- **Humans respond to stories.** Stories are the best way to communicate to people's hearts and minds, and create inspiration.
- **A story tailored to your teams must follow basic elements and include the Why.** You have to unite the organization as the protagonist in completing the task at hand to fulfill the grander purpose.
- **A story tailored to your peers paints a picture to solve a problem.** It may follow some of the basic elements, but it may not relate their roles back to the Why.
- **A story tailored to your leaders simply tells the whole story.** It opens with the punchline and includes the contextual background, full description of the situation, and the proposed or current solution to communicate more effectively and holistically.

Commitment

Inspiration is the outcome of engagement, and commitment is one of the outcomes of inspiration. When you can get people not only by your side but to follow you to the ends of the Earth, you can truly move the many mountains ahead of you. This can only be done through building commitment.

This *can't* be done with compliance. Nobody who is just doing something because you said so is willing to give more than the bare minimum. You need a team of highly-motivated and dedicated people, not drones. An organization's purpose can't be fulfilled by employees who are only going through the motions.

Commitment is the key to unlocking the magic, achieving innovation, and driving the next level of performance. It's one of the most valuable assets a leader can ever earn and should be treated like gold. It's also a two-way street—you have to be committed to guiding and bettering your teams just as much as they are committed to striding forward in the path you've led them. Their commitment can never be taken for granted.

Historically, significant changes in any of the previously-mentioned areas were held close to the vest. The notion of confidentiality generally led the depth of information shared and defined the number of people engaged along the way. This was primarily done as a measure of caution in ensuring that nothing was leaked ahead of time. But the unintended consequence of this exclusion was that people weren't given the time to commit, and instead were forced to be compliant. Humans need time to process and adjust to change, much less become committed to it. By including them on the journey, they can acclimate and commit. By the way, in this day and age, it's better to stop questioning if something is going to leak and instead just prepare for it…it's inevitable. You need to build contingency plans to prepare for that event instead of being too protective and putting your team members behind the 8-ball. Bravery before perfection, exceptions to the side.

An individual's journey to committing to a new path can be broken down into five distinct stages: Awareness, Understanding, Buy-In, Ownership, and finally Engagement. The Commitment Model below depicts the journey.

The Commitment Model

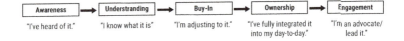

As you can see, it starts at Awareness. This is when an individual initially hears about a new project, innovation, change, etcetera. Their familiarity with what's to come is likely about as much as when you first see a billboard for a new blockbuster while you're driving down the road. They may have the general idea of what's going on based on that cursory information, but it's not specific or substantial enough for them to care too much yet. It is what it is—a static billboard that might capture *x* percent of the people driving by, but has no context or purpose. With no real knowledge of the details, they are not engaged or attached. However, this will soon change.

Moving into Understanding, where they're learning more about it and starting to gain a more in-depth comprehension of *exactly* what's going on. Going back to my movie metaphor, this would be at the same point where you watch the trailer. You don't necessarily know where it will all go—and usually, nobody does in these things—but you have most of the available information.

Now comes the Buy-In. They not only recognize that a change is imminent and know what they can about it, but they're actually starting to adapt to it too. They've looked at the billboard, seen the trailer, and now, they're going to go watch it. They're changing the way they work and think to get used to this new change and make it a part of their daily life. This adjustment period may take more time and have some bumps, sure, but this is the critical midpoint in the journey that every individual has to reach along the way to commitment.

This is when we get to Ownership—they've seen the billboard, viewed the trailer, watched the movie, and they love it! They know the ins and outs of the new change and have adopted it in their day-to-day. It's no longer some unknown territory on the horizon, it's become mostly familiar territory they feel they are a part of. But the commitment journey isn't quite complete.

Finally, it all leads to Engagement. Now the student has become the master, and they are leading others down the path they have taken themselves to commit to this change too. The same way you would tell all of your friends about how much you love this new movie, those who have reached Engagement have joined the efforts to get the rest of the organization on board are now advocating this new change to those around them. *That* is the pinnacle of commitment.

When you build true commitment with one person, it immediately becomes a multiplier. They'll turn around and build commitment with one more person, and then they'll go build commitment with yet another person...and so on. Commitment engenders more commitment, and unites the organization to this "new thing" in a way that not many other things can. It builds exponentially and is one of the most powerful forces within your organization.

So, how do we lead people through these five stages? While the answer is easier said than done, it is *really* easy to say—engagement, inclusion, and inspiration. But there are no shortcuts (sorry!). You have to connect with them authentically, bring them in on the journey as soon as possible, and create continuous inspiration as they go along with you. This is the only way to build commitment but, once you have and work to keep it, you can do just about anything.

Key Takeaways

- **Commitment is the outcome of inspiration.** When someone is inspired to take your path, they give it their all and create magic.

- **Commitment is one of the most valuable assets you can create.** A compliant individual will not do nearly as much as a committed one, and the only way to fulfill the purpose is through building commitment.

- **The journey to commitment can be broken down into five stages.** Awareness, Understanding, Buy-In, Ownership, and Engagement are the key points along someone's journey to committing to something.

- **Once someone is committed, they'll get others to commit too.** Since they become advocates, commitment is built on an exponential scale.

- **You can only build commitment through engagement, inclusion, and continuous inspiration.** This is the simple answer, but it isn't easy.

Summary

- Making work fun is about tending to the physical and emotional environment, and giving recognition and appreciation at the right times.

- Creating inspiration is about understanding your company's Why for yourself, and then connecting everyone at every level to the purpose.

- Telling the right story is how a leader can communicate with people's hearts and minds at a much deeper level and get them excited to fulfill the organization's purpose.

- Commitment is the outcome of inspiration. Engagement, inclusion, and continuous inspiration is the only way to build commitment, but it is one of the most powerful forces you can have as a leader.

LEAD

Lead

"to direct on a course or in a direction"

Introduction

The equation is pretty simple:

> **Engage + Inspire = Lead**

You get people engaged, inspire them, and then you lead them. And in the words of the wise Yoda, "Do or do not. There is no try." You either lead, or you don't.

THE END

Nah, I'm just kidding...I wish it was really that easy! And I hope that reading this book helps you in some way, but this is by no means a one-and-done guide to becoming an inspirational leader. Like we've talked about, it's a lifelong journey that looks different for everyone. There isn't one correct and surefire path here.

As I've been writing this book in retirement, I've had the time and opportunity to reflect on my past and use what I've experienced and learned to propel myself into the future. Most significantly, I've been thinking about those three words—engage, inspire, lead—and I've come to realize that it's an input/output operation. When we engage and inspire, we are extending our inner selves out to others. That's what we're willing to put in. Then, when others recognize our input and allow us to guide them down the path, that's the output—leading. The way I see it, the art of leadership has to be jump-started first by some serious, vulnerable input on your part through reflection and realization.

Like I've said, it can be dangerous to spend too long looking back, but understanding how you have gotten to where you are is the only way to set the course for where you're going. Think about what has come to define who you are—as a person, neighbor, friend, spouse, parent, sibling... and leader. What were your formative experiences? Which influences were most impactful? Who inspired you the most? Although prying deeply into yourself can be uncomfortable, if not even a bit painful at times, asking these kinds of questions is how you develop self-awareness, a necessary ingredient in inspirational leadership.

Now, realization—we all have to realize and fully comprehend the weight that our role carries. Not that I'm saying anything new, though. Luke 12:48 noted that "From everyone who has been given much, much will be demanded; and from the one who has been entrusted with much, much more will be asked." Or, as Uncle Ben told Peter Parker in *Spider Man*, "With great power comes great responsibilities." We can't ever forget the obligation we have to fulfill in our position.

I believe, first and foremost, we have to recognize what an absolute privilege it is to be a leader. To lead an organization as large as Walt Disney World and be a part of the most talented and hardworking team of cast members at the largest entertainment destination in the world was an incredible honor. But that honor also came with a sometimes overwhelming list of duties on a significant scale. In the last few years of my career, I was responsible for over 50,000 cast members and leaders tasked with delivering lifelong experiences to tens of millions of guests each and every year, not to mention answering to my own leaders and fulfilling our obligations to shareholders. *Over fifty thousand cast members...tens of millions of guests...literally making magic.* Daunting, as I think about it.

At the bare minimum, leaders are tasked with what I call "delivering the base," or producing the expectations with operational excellence. In my business, delivering the base meant creating our famous experiences while practicing safety, courtesy, inclusion, show, and efficiency. No pressure...

But I came to realize that while this was a big responsibility, my responsibility for others was even bigger. Everyone at the organization is asked to give no less than 100% in their individual roles each and every day to help fulfill the organization's purpose. In turn, I had the careers and livelihoods of so many extraordinary people who had committed themselves to what they do. If I failed, I failed *them*. That was the real pressure.

The pressure was positive, though. While it might sound obvious, I was personally fueled by realizing what was on the line and that we were all one great big team working hand-in-hand on greater and greater challenges. What we did, we did together, and that fact motivated me unlike anything else.

Leading is the culmination of engagement and inspiration, but leadership really starts from within. By understanding the privilege you've been given and the responsibilities you have as a result, you can truly and fully commit to becoming an inspirational leader. Because really, you aren't doing it for the benefit of your own career—you're doing it for the people who have entrusted themselves to your direction. That's the real reason for all of this.

Now that you have a team committed to following your path, it's on you to be the leader that they deserve. In this section, we'll discuss the philosophies I believe you need to continue building commitment and creating inspiration while delivering the base and driving performance at the highest levels possible.

Key Takeaways

- **Engagement + Inspiration = Leadership.** When you have engaged and inspired your team, they will ultimately allow you to lead them.

- **Leadership starts from within.** You have to reflect on how you became who you are today and realize the true weight of leadership.

- **Leadership is a great privilege and responsibility.** You are responsible for other people's livelihoods and careers.

- **Ultimately, leadership is about others, not yourself.** While the position might have career benefits, your real motivation should come from the people you are responsible for.

Clarity, Unity, and Agility

I would be remiss if I didn't open this section by crediting the book this concept originally came from, *Strategic Speed: Mobilize People, Accelerate Execution*. I originally read this around 2005, when we were focusing on a "One Disney" mindset and strengthening connections between the sites. For the first time, leaders from Disneyland and Disney World sat down to share strategies. As part of this exercise in cross pollination, we read this book, which greatly resonated with me.

In the book, they assert that clarity, unity, and agility are three factors that get people to move toward the end goal quicker. However, as ideas that are spread from person to person do, my interpretation of this is a little bit different. I look at it like this—clarity creates unity and enables agility, which drives teams to get to the end destination faster. For me, it all starts with clarity.

When you clearly articulate your expectations and goals, the entire team will be set on the right path and nobody will go astray. If everyone knows where they're going without any question or room for misunderstanding, there's nothing to do but simply go. And when you don't have to constantly regroup lost and confused teams, you get there faster than ever. That's pretty self-evident.

On the other hand, an absence of upfront clarity will create room for increasing chaos down the chain of command. One vague word in a message from the top could result in a Wild

Wild West on the frontlines, with everyone doing their own thing and essentially wasting energy driven from that lack of clarity. I really can't overstate how important it is for top-level leadership to get together, create one message, and communicate it as explicitly and completely as possible.

Think about the Liberty Bell and the famous crack running down it.[9] The crack starts fairly small at the top, but it grows bigger and bigger the further it goes. I don't know the actual science behind why that physically happened, but it's the same thing in organization—what starts as a small split between the message given and how it was received will eventually create total havoc down the line.

You've probably played Telephone back in elementary school. You stand in a line and whisper a message from the front to the back. Almost always, what the first person said and the last person heard are going to be two very, very different things. "I went to the store last night" can turn into "I robbed a bank this morning" in just one round. It's funny as a game, but the real-life consequences can be disastrous. You need to ensure what you say is so crystal-clear and explicit that nothing can be lost in translation. Ambiguity is your enemy here.

I should also mention that oftentimes, there's a lack of clarity in organizational design and reporting relationships. This lack of clarity generally surfaces when there's an attempt to use dual-reporting lines. If you've ever had the pleasure of a

---

9   I'd also be remiss if I didn't credit Scot Reynolds, my colleague, for this idea.

dual-reporting relationship, you'll know exactly what I mean. In my experience, dual-reporting relationships are often unnecessary and, in many cases, indicate a lack of trust within the organization. These often come in the form of dual hard lines or dual dotted lines. Hard lines are just that—defined, drawn-in-the-sand lines of whom you report to and for what. Dotted lines are the ambiguous, semi-formal arrangements where someone will check in on someone else's direct report. When someone creates a dotted line report, they're usually saying, "I don't think you're going to do your job if I don't keep an eye on you." It leads to a confusing and often frustrating situation wherein a report is split between two leaders to answer to and two leaders are both responsible—to varying lengths—for the same direct report.

One of the funniest quotes I've heard regarding dual-reporting relationships is from Jeff Vahle. He asked me the following: "If you were on a boat out at sea and suddenly fell off, would you want someone to throw you a life ring connected to a dotted line or a hard line?" That still cracks me up today.

It's just as easy to get your teams moving together as it is to get them running in different directions. When top-level leaders communicate with total clarity—with no margin of error or gray area for interpretation—teams will be united under the message and work faster with no deviation from the original plan, while being nimble and agile along the way. But when there's a lack of clarity at the top, an ever-widening crack will run through the organization, leading to a fatal fissure on the frontlines. To get everyone on the same page and avoid the Wild Wild West, all you have to do is communicate in a precise, complete, and thorough way. It really is that simple.

Key Takeaways

- **Clarity creates unity and enables agility.** You can get your teams together and move toward the destination faster, while being nimble and agile along the way.

- **A lack of clarity at the top will create chaos at the front line.** When the message has any ambiguity, misinterpretation will only get worse and worse down the chain of command.

- **Clear, upfront communication about your destination gets you there faster.** This is how you can unite your teams, keep them from going wayward, and get everybody working to reach the goal.

Strengthen Your Core

Let me answer the question you're probably asking now—*no*, we're not talking about doing situps or getting a 6-pack here. While abdominal strength is always good, the core we need to focus on is that of your organization. Here, "strengthening your core" refers to the importance of continued focus on delivering the base.

Each and every day, your organization has to deliver its base. That's just how economics works. Success can be determined simply by whether the organization has performed its most elemental function. If a restaurant served meals, a theater screened a film, a dry cleaner washed clothes, or a hospital treated patients, then they have undoubtedly delivered their base and, as a result, succeeded…if only for that day.

While our organization at Disney runs across so many lines of business, we know we've succeeded when we create memories for guests. If I walk by Ariel's Grotto and see a little kid chatting excitedly with the Little Mermaid herself, I know we've delivered our base. There are so many different things going on across the property at the same time, but it all comes together to make moments that guests will remember for a lifetime. That's our base, delivered.

Of course, you have to be forward-thinking and strive for continuous innovation. If you narrow your focus to just what's going on each day on the front lines, your organization will not have much of a future. However, you need to always keep your eye on the core. Without a focus on the organization's foundation and what it does, you will eventually lose sight of that entirely and become aimless.

What may surprise you is this is much easier said than done. The further you grow within an organization and are tasked with the "higher-level" responsibilities, the further you get from focusing on the core of the organization. Our core has always been legendary guest service. It's much easier for someone directly serving the guests each and every day—the cast members who operate rides, ring up purchases, take food orders, keep the streets clean, etcetera—to focus on our core than it is for someone who's sitting in an office most of the day.

At the same time, a leader really can't focus as deeply on the core as someone on the front line does. Because unlike someone on the front line, a leader must also focus on the future and innovation. The person running a popcorn cart doesn't have to concern themselves with transforming the business, since that's quite literally someone else's job—yours. As your responsibilities increase, your attention is demanded in more and more places. You only have two eyes, and it's admittedly challenging to keep them on everything at once.

Innovation is obviously important, and it's obviously on the leaders to keep the organization moving forward. But a leader also can't just think about what *could* be and neglect what it already *is*. If you spend too much time chasing shiny objects and not enough time paying attention to the core, the organization can start to fall apart.

Like so many things in life and leadership, the focus between your core and innovation is a fine line that you, as a leader, have to manage. Always look to the future and think innovatively, but never lose sight of your core and ensure your organization is always delivering its base. It's not one or the other here—it's both, always. As high as you may climb within the ranks and as lofty as your responsibilities may get, never get too detached from the day-to-day front lines. That's the core of your organization, and you can't forget it.

Key Takeaways

- **Your business is successful each day only if it delivers its base.** It must perform its most basic function in order to continue.

- **You always need to keep an eye on your organization's core.** This foundation, if lost, will lead to your organization becoming aimless and adrift.

- **As a leader, you become removed from the front lines and tasked with innovative thinking.** This makes it more challenging to continue a focus on the core as well.

- **You need to divide your attention between innovation and the core.** By seeing what it is while also thinking about what it could be, you can transform the business.

Lead with a Holistic Mindset

So we've just covered the importance of the organization's core. Delivering the base each and every day is important, got it. Now let's look at the other side of that coin—you can't *just* focus on vertical execution. As a leader, you have to think holistically.

Holistic thinking is distinctly a leader's responsibility. Your frontline workers will largely be focused on fulfilling the purpose in their role and don't really need to consider the implications beyond their area. And customers definitely aren't thinking about anything more than the end result you are giving them. I have said a million times—and I think I've actually permanently borrowed this quote from Meg: "Guests don't care about the org charts." The details don't matter to them—all they want is a seamless experience. It's your job to figure out how to create one.

Remember, your business card calls out your expertise, but it doesn't really describe what you do. And *everything* you do feeds back into the purpose. Unlike those on the front lines, everything you do has multipliers far beyond the immediate here and now. Each act on your level, however seemingly small, will have effects further than the supposed parameters. So naturally, you have to consider the implications your decisions will have on the broader organization.

As a leader, you are in an incredible position to make an impact on others. When you are conscious of this fact and act meaningfully, you can create so much positivity and inspiration within your organization and beyond. At the same time, your actions can have inadvertent consequences for others if you are not being thoughtful and conscientious of your power. This is why you have to understand both the end-to-end experience and how your decisions will affect those within the organization at all levels, your customers or guests, and the ultimate business results. A holistic mindset is the only way to fully understand all these potential effects and make the best decision as a result.

To be able to think holistically, you first have to get a good grasp on two things— Mastery and Command, and Systems and Critical Thinking. These concepts work hand-in-hand to give you the full view of your Operations and complete understanding of how your individual actions will reverberate throughout the organization.

Mastery and Command happens when you understand both how all the different areas of your organization work together *and* what to do with each to make the right impact on the other. Basically, if you're a captain standing at the bridge of a ship, you not only know what all the dials are and how they affect each other, but you also know when and how much to turn every single one. This takes some serious RIKCing, among so many other things, and a lot of time to confidently take control like this. But as a leader who affects others, you have to gain Mastery and Command to be a fully-effective leader.

Of course, I should specify that Mastery and Command doesn't mean becoming the absolute all-around expert. You can't know every single thing about everything, and you aren't expected to. It's actually impossible to completely master everything, and to learn all of that information is not the best use of a leader's time.

When I was in charge of all aspects of Operations at the WDW property, I most definitely did not know every single thing about all that went on. I had a solid understanding of each line of business, of course, but with the exception of Operations, I was not the expert of them. I couldn't tell you exactly how many Audio-Animatronics there are in Spaceship Earth, the price of a caramel apple at Main Street Confectionary, or what brand of mattresses we have in the Grand Floridian—and if I did, that'd only tell you I wasn't focusing on the right things.

As a leader, you can't attain complete and total expertise of everything within your organization. Instead, you have to surround yourself with subject experts to knit all that information together so you can make the best decisions. Your team will offer small, detailed pieces of knowledge, and you need to understand enough of it to be able to build the big picture.

You may have heard the popular saying, "Jack of all trades and master of none," which most people understand to mean that someone with a broad knowledge base doesn't have any real expertise. Following this logic, you may draw the conclusion that it's better to be really knowledgeable at one thing than familiar with many.

However, what you may not know is this is only the first half of the saying. Many people conveniently leave out the last part, which completely changes the meaning. The whole saying goes, "Jack of all trades and master of none, but oftentimes better than a master of one." As you can see, the original meaning was totally different from the way we understand it today. With this in mind, understanding many things on a surface level may actually be better than knowing only one thing in-depth. These are two opposing takes here.

With Mastery and Command, I really think leaders should strive to be an expert in their core area and gain at least a rudimentary grasp on everything else. You need to know enough to understand what your team of experts are telling you and be able to make the big-picture decisions from there. That, in my opinion, is Master and Command, not to be confused with Command and Control.

Once you've built that into your leadership mindset, you also want to start to invest in Systems and Critical Thinking. This is when you fully understand how every aspect of the organization in tandem works together to create the final result and can then make decisions through that end-to-end mindframe. While I didn't yet have the word for it then, I first experienced Systems and Critical Thinking back in my restaurant days. Kitchens work a lot like an assembly line—you got your hot side grilling and frying the meat, stove working the pastas and sauces, cold side prepping salads, etcetera. As a kid, I'd marvel at how all that madness—knives chopping furiously, cooks shouting at each other, the occasional cloud of smoke erupting from something left too long on the pan—magically came together to turn orders on a ticket into meals on a plate.

It also seems impossible, yet kitchen staff can quickly and predictably churn out the same dish every single time by working this way. None of them are creating the product from end to end, but all of them are able to *think* end-to-end. If grill is down, cold side knows they can't complete their Steak Salad order. And if stove runs behind, grill won't have any spaghetti for their Chicken Parmigiana. The cooks on the line, the dishwashers in the pit, the servers by the tables, and the hosts at the door all know that if one aspect is down, the whole business grinds to a halt.

You might not be in a restaurant, but your organization works the same way—everyone needs everybody, nobody can really work alone. There is no one aspect of a business that can single-handedly deliver the base and fulfill the purpose. There is *always* some connection to other areas to get things done.

Systems are just as interconnected on the larger scale, perhaps even more so. The larger your organization is, the more systems you'll have working together. And the more systems you have working together, the more that can go wrong. You get a lot more dials that you have to pay attention to, or you will inevitably experience a serious issue that affects the entire end result.

For example, think about the arrival experience at Disney. A guest may only ever think about the moment they tap their Magic Band at the touch point and enter the park, but there's actually so much more that goes into that moment. First, you've got people coming to the property by resort buses or cars. That means at least the bus system and parking system have to work together. Then, all these people arriving converge on the ferry boats, Monorails, Skyliner, or in pedestrian traffic to get to the gates. This isn't even to mention the toll plaza, ticketing, and river boats that a guest may use along the way. All told, it takes many different systems working together along the way to get guests onto the property and into the parks.

If any one of these systems were to go down at any point, it could very easily cause a humongous backup of guests and affect the whole organization if it were not quickly and adequately addressed. Nothing is done in isolation, so you have to contemplate and regulate the many systems to prevent a blip in one area from creating a trainwreck throughout the entire organization.

When you make decisions for one area, you also have to think about where it links up to others and how it could affect them (because, believe me, it will). While something might make sense for one area, it may overall not be conducive for the entirety. I can tell you this with certainty, because I've seen exactly how something like this plays out.

One summer not too long ago, I got a note from Tom Staggs who asked me this wonderful question: "Can you tell me more about the poop sweets for sale at Disney's Animal Kingdom?" Poop? Sweets?! The national headline that day—"Disney is Now Selling Poop." Wonderful.

And what was wonderful is that I had no clue what he was asking about, so I told him I'd get the scoop on the poop (sort of). FYI, we weren't *actually* selling poop. As it turns out, somebody in Harambe Village Merchandise thought it'd be fun to sell poop-themed treats in Zuri's Sweet Shop. For only $3.99, you could get candy made to look exceedingly like real-life animal droppings. You even had your choice of four different flavors—tamarin, giraffe, elephant, and hippo. With all the articles written about this, there didn't seem to be any consensus for which flavor was best.

While the poop thing was admittedly a pretty cool idea that worked in isolation at Animal Kingdom—sales weren't bad—it didn't really bode well with the rest of WDW. I mean, could you imagine how that'd go down if we sold it in the World Showcase or on Main Street? If a contrarian had been engaged early on and the team elected to identify any unintended consequences, they likely would have realized that selling poop—even delicious poop made out of chocolate and peanut butter—did not fit with the rest of the brand. There's plenty of poop happening out of our control as it is, so we didn't need to add to it. Lesson learned, but I think the team would agree that we exited the whole ordeal smoothly, so to speak. This is why we can't think in silos.

What one system does impacts the rest, so you always have to ensure what you're doing is consistent with the broader organization.

Thinking holistically also means thinking things all the way through. That's the thing about end-to-end thinking—you've actually got to consider each part of the process as fully and carefully as the last. It's not beginning-to-middle thinking, or middle-to-end. You have to think about what it takes to get from Point A to Point B and everything that happens in between. If you don't, you'll inevitably miss something that will come back to bite you.

I've actually got another story for this one, also in Animal Kingdom. One day during pre-opening, I was on a specialized vehicle expressly built to take VIP/dignitary guests onto the Kilimanjaro Safaris Savannah. I was hosting the president of Walt Disney World Resort, the Chairman of Parks & Resorts, and, oddly enough, Newt Gingrich[10]. Before we went out, someone was supposed to ride ahead and ensure the path was clear for guests, particularly the finality segment, which has an approximately three-foot section of water simulating a flooding that should have been drained prior to our arrival. Well, it just so happened that this time, when I was riding with three VIPs, this protocol had been neglected. And, it just so happened that this time, that part of the path was indeed flooded. And, it was absolutely impossible to turn the vehicle around.

---

10 A former Representative from Georgia who served as the 50th Speaker of the House.

Keep in mind, we were not in the typical ride vehicle designed to drive through this water. We were in a van that sat a lot lower and should not have been able to make it through. There was a pretty good chance the van could get stuck in the water.

If the due diligence had been done, this problem would've been discovered and drained without a second thought. But since that didn't happen, I was in a pickle and had to choose whether to wait out there for assistance or to drive the vehicle through it. I chose the latter, which luckily worked out, but in hindsight, was a very risky decision. The whole situation could've been so easily avoided if we had simply done the due diligence—ride the ride path.

From then on, Ride the Ride Path became a "Jimism" around thorough preparation and readiness that I preached to others. And all Ride the Ride Path means is to prepare for what's to come and pay attention to detail. You have to do your best to see the path ahead and ensure it's clear before you lead anyone down it. There will always be unexpected obstacles that get in the way, of course, but you at least need to check for anything obvious beforehand...like, you know, a flooded area.

Leaders leave larger footprints than many expect, one that extends beyond their direct reports and areas. Whether you see it or not, every organization is interconnected and can't really work in silos. Since it takes each and every aspect of the business to deliver the final results, you have to think holistically and from end to end. And, you have to gain both Mastery and Command and Systems and Critical Thinking to do so. And that takes time leveraging and engaging with your teams—your teams, your peers, and your leaders—and demonstrating your Mastery and Command and Systems and Critical Thinking to build credibility and their confidence in you.

While this is admittedly quite a bit of effort and thought, it's also quite literally what you signed up for. Your impact as a leader—at least, as an effective and inspirational one—runs deep and spreads wide throughout the organization. It's a strength you have to be cognizant of at all times. But by adopting a holistic mindset and considering all potential implications, you can utilize this strength to create the largest, most positive effect you can.

Key Takeaways

- **Leaders are uniquely tasked with thinking vertically AND horizontally.** It's quite literally your job to focus on delivering the base, optimizing the base, and innovating, while ensuring the broader organization is all interconnected, all of the time.

- **You have to think holistically.** You have to thoroughly consider how your decisions will impact those within the organization, guests/customers, and business results. Tap into your contrarian to really make sure you're thinking all the way through.

- **To think holistically, you have to gain Mastery and Command and Systems and Critical Thinking.** These two concepts are the only way to truly see the end-to-end.

- **Mastery and Command is knowing how each dial affects the other and when to turn each one and to what degree.** You have to have deep knowledge of how your organization runs in each aspect to gain this. Remember that the closer you are to the front lines, the closer you are to the truth, so be sure to tap into the experts that make it all happen.

- **Systems and Critical Thinking is understanding how the lines of business work together and how your decisions will impact each one.** Nobody can single-handedly deliver the final result, so you have to see how they work together and how doing something in one area will affect another.

- **Ride the Ride Path means doing your homework and checking for what's ahead.** While we can't predict exactly what will happen, you have to take an end-to-end perspective to look for and clear any obvious obstacles.

Leading with a Transformative Mindset

I've probably said the word a few too many times already, so I guess there's no real harm in saying it again—innovation and transformation is a requirement for continued success in today's rapidly-evolving world. The world moves quickly, and if you don't keep up, your organization will be left behind to die in its wake. Every leader is looking to innovate, but many don't actually understand everything that has to happen ahead of innovation. There are many courses to consume before getting to that main entree, and we'll be talking about what those are in this section.

So, we all know the end goal—we want to innovate and take our organizations to the next level. We want to reinvent and transform the experience we deliver to our guests. Now, let's work backward. Before you can reinvent the experience, you have to make sure the business is running really well to begin with and in its best form. Try as you might, you can't skip these steps. It's all well and good to put newer and better sails on your boat, sure, but if you don't address the giant hole in the hull, you will eventually sink. Prerequisites are prerequisites for a reason—you have to build on what you have to transform it to what you want it to be.

First step: ensure the business is already running really really well. Your business needs to be in the right shape to even start to head down the innovation track. If there are pressing issues and glaring problems in the organization, you won't be in any place for transformation until everything is resolved. Again, a sinking ship doesn't really benefit from any upgrades if they don't fix the leaks below. Assess your organization—holistically and thoroughly—and determine if attention is needed anywhere else before you proceed.

Let's say your organization is a counter-service restaurant chain. You need to audit how the business is currently running to ensure the bare minimum is being met—is the food served correctly, are the front-facing employees practicing customer service, are the locations clean, etcetera. If, say, your place of business is a constant source of listeria outbreaks, well, then you need to get that fixed before you can continue. Only once you know everything is running as it should can you move forward.

Okay, no glaring problems in the business. Great. Now it's time to start thinking about efficiency. Efficiency is usually synonymous with "cost management," and I am *not* a fan of solely focusing on efficiency through that perspective. The perspective should be, how can we make Operations run as productively as possible? This is where some people might start to make mistakes with short-sighted cost-cutting measures.

If you have two cashiers at the counter and decide to only have one working at a time, closing that second register may seem like it'd save you money, but it actually is going to cost you *more* in the long run. You won't have to pay an extra employee, but your customer's wait times will increase. And I of all people can tell you, you want to keep those wait times down as much as possible because that's what people remember—long lines...not the great food they get at the end of them.

If your customers have to wait longer to place an order, they're more likely to leave and go to the other place next door instead. So all you've done is redirect the money you would have paid for the cashier into lost profit. What do you think costs you more, an hourly wage or the line of people who walked out the door?

Other supposedly "efficient" measures might actually save you money, true, but they cost you in other ways. At Disney, it would technically be efficient to have fewer character meet-and-greets. But, that would take away from the overall experience for our guests. Is it still a magical memory if you went to Disney and didn't get to meet one of the princesses? Probably, but it's just not *as* magical without it. When you get rid of certain perceived "extra" elements of what you deliver to your guests or customers, you ultimately detract from the overall quality and experience of it. After all, people have high expectations for Disney, and our charter is to always go above and beyond.

Without those special factors that no one else was offering, you lose affinity and, ultimately, business. When an efficiency measure ends up detracting from your value proposition, it's really not efficient at all.

At its core, efficiency is ensuring everything is running at the budgeted levels, the right throughputs, and with minimal waste in the system. That often means standardizing things, like limiting each restaurant's choice of types of olive oils from ~70 to ~10 at the most. Now, this example may sound myopic, but when you lead a resort destination that has literally hundreds of restaurants, the impact of something like this is actually quite significant on the supply chain. And if you multiply that across other seemingly small things, they end up being scarily big from a cost perspective.

All it takes to make the distinction between a detractive measure and an efficient one is to consider its long-term, end-to-end impact. Will the organization continue to deliver the same high-value result to the guest or customer? If so, it's probably the right move.

Efficiency is important, but if it's an organization's sole or primary focus, it's somewhat short-sighted. However, it is a critical foundational element to set before moving to optimization. All of these efforts ultimately prime your organization for transformation. When your organization is doing everything well, you can start to see how you can do things even *better*.

Optimization is all about how you can make better use of your resources rather than figuring ways to cut or stretch them at the expense of quality. For instance, let's say you've looked around in your restaurant and realize your two cashiers are ringing in orders on horrifically outdated and slow Point of Sale (POS) systems. The register's system takes several minutes to process each order, minutes the customers spend standing awkwardly at the counter and minutes the cooks have to wait before they know what they're making. As you see all this taking place, you think to yourself, "There's got to be a better way of doing this." And there definitely is.

You do your research and find out there's a newer and faster program you can use on the POS systems instead. It's still the same interface and runs on the same registers—not much extra training, no real preparation, no more resources spent beyond the program license and an installation. You implement the update, and things are immediately better. Orders are taken without technical delay, customers wait less, and food comes out faster. It's a meaningful win for Operations, and all it took was an attentive eye and a willingness to improve.

Another optimization effort could be restructuring your current queue lines that expand into your area of development into creative switchback lines, like how we do at Disney, to save space in your restaurant and reallocate it into more seating for customers, which increases your capacity and subsequent sales. Or, you might realize it'd be better to place bottled drinks in a cooler at the counter rather than in the back so customers can see what you offer, are more likely to buy a drink, and don't have to wait for an employee to go back and grab it after they order.

While these examples may be relatively academic for many of you, the point of this is the mindset. When you are not comfortable with the status quo and are willing to take on this optimization perspective, you can find all kinds of ways to update and improve your current Operations.

At this point, we've made the business the best it could be in its current form. When you've established your foundation of efficiency and optimization, you're finally ready for the fun stuff—innovation and transformation. These aren't just simple upgrades or small improvements. Way too many people jump into these efforts without fully understanding how massive of an undertaking it really is, and they almost inevitably end up failing as a result. Don't underestimate how much time and effort it's really going to take. You're not just trying to improve the machine here—you're trying to transform it completely.

In your restaurant, that would be like deciding that your ordering system has to be redesigned completely. You've seen that customers don't like waiting, having to talk to a cashier, and the lack of customization. In short, their experience could be better. You've identified their friction points and created solutions for them—instead of placing an order with a cashier at the counter, why can't they just place it directly and have options to make their order exactly how they want it? You get rid of the registers entirely and retrain the cashiers to work in different functions. Instead, you install kiosks where customers can just walk up, choose and customize what they want from the menu, pay, take a number, and sit at a table for their order to be called, all without having to stand in line or have a lengthy back-and-forth to communicate what they want to someone else.

This change is good, but what if they don't want to wait at all? That's when you decide to launch an app for mobile orders. Now, customers can choose what they want and set a pickup time. They can walk right in, grab their bag from a clearly-labeled shelf of orders, and be on their way. This is a much quicker and more convenient choice than you'd ever offered before.

Of course, it's much easier said than done—you'll have to retrain staff, restructure the kitchens to handle these different orders, and spend no small chunk of money to get this done. But once you've brought your restaurant to this next level, you'll add an enormous extra value to what you offer customers and keep up, or even beat, your competitors. You can't put a price tag on something like that.

Sooner or later, you will have to transform your business. You can do this either proactively or reactively. When you commit to proactive transformation, you give yourself the time and budgeted resources to make it happen and be successful. While the necessity of transformation may not be immediately apparent, you'll eventually come to see just how important it is for the survival of your business.

The design and implementation of a mobile ordering system may not have seemed to "pay off" in the beginning. I can say that when we introduced mobile ordering at WDW, only a percentage of our guests actually used it. The food service industry as a whole didn't seem to "need" a mobile ordering system when it first became adopted as a transformative strategy. However, I'm sure you can imagine when mobile ordering became an absolute necessity for businesses—the COVID-19 pandemic.

In a situation where restaurants needed to safely serve their customers in the face of a public health crisis, mobile ordering allowed them to still conduct business while reducing exposure risk as much as possible. The organizations that had undergone proactive transformation already had the system in place and could quickly pivot. On the other hand, the organizations that hadn't yet done so had to transform *reactively*. A reactive transformation is a rush job prompted by the pressures of an external situation. An organization may not have the time and resources at the ready when they're forced to undergo the transformation, which often makes the endeavor 10x harder and at a much higher cost than when it's planned. And oftentimes, a reactive transformation is late to the party. This can unfortunately spell the death of an organization.

Transforming your business takes a dedicated focus, dedicated resources, and a large upfront investment to sustain it. And the results can't always be measured quantitatively right away. You really have to take the long view and understand how while, yes, you might not get an immediate payoff, the results over time will grow exponentially. Aside from that, innovation and transformation is the only way to continue to succeed and grow. There's really no other way to predict and navigate the changing tides, so an organization will have to innovate to keep up no matter what.

Innovation and transformation is a must, but it's only the surface. You have to first get your organization to the point where it's *ready* to be transformed before you actually can. And you can't get to that point without putting in the unglamorous work. Only when your business is running at the best it can in its current form can you then transform it into a different one entirely. By staying connected to current Operations and staying open to change, you can make your organization ready for transformation.

Key Takeaways

- **There are prerequisites to innovation and transformation that you can't skip.** Before you can transform the business, you have to ensure it's running well and as best as it currently can.

- **Efficiency efforts are typically more short-sighted, but they shouldn't detract from your value proposition.** If you choose to do something purely for cost-cutting, you'll end up lowering the overall quality of what you deliver to customers. This may include some standardization to avoid resource wastage.

- **Optimization is about improving current Operations.** This is all about looking at how you are currently doing things and see if they can be done better in some way.

- **You are ready for innovation and transformation only when your organization is at the best it can currently be.** Skipping this step will only lead to failure.

- **Transforming your business is a long-term investment that has to be sustained.** You have to dedicate time, resource, and focus just toward these efforts and understand that your ROI comes over years and years.

- **Innovation and transformation is the only way to keep up.** The market changes quickly, and if you don't change with it, your organization will eventually get left behind.

Heritage and Tradition

I'm probably beating a dead horse at this point, but I'll say it again—while looking in the past for too long can be dangerous, reflecting back on how you've gotten to where you are today is crucial in setting the next destination and retaining your roots along the way. As Socrates said thousands of years ago, "Know thyself." Or, as the spirit of Mufasa told Simba in *The Lion King*, "Remember who you are." Connecting to where you came from is a part of the journey, but there is a fine line between honoring your heritage and being stuck in the past.

The heritage of an organization is immensely important, but it can be misused. On one hand, losing a hold of the foundation can cause the organization to forget themselves and become aimless amidst change. It's very, very hard to evolve a business if you don't have a grasp on its origins. How are you supposed to take it to the next level if you don't understand the level you're currently on or started at? And even if you can continue to innovate without remembering the heritage, you lose sight of the original purpose. So, in a way, forgetting the heritage will make everything accomplished, well, a moot point.

However, there has to be a self-imposed limit on looking back. Be fueled by your foundation, but don't let it hold you back. And it's very easy to get held back by your past if you let it. If you grow too comfortable doing things how you've always done them, you'll eventually be unable to change and your business will slowly die. You can't shut your mind off from considering fresh takes and new ideas—that's how you kill innovation.

Walt himself said it best: "In this volatile business of ours, we can ill afford to rest on our laurels, even to pause in retrospect. Times and conditions change so rapidly that we must keep our aim constantly focused on the future." This, in fact, is the essence of innovation and transformation. The world moves so quickly that we can all easily fall behind if we stop to look back for too long. The heritage should be in the back of your mind, while the future should take the forefront. That's the only way forward, after all.

Now, the Disney organization has changed so often and so rapidly that you may be questioning whether we have ever honored our heritage and traditions. Well, first of all, we literally have an orientation class for new cast members called Traditions. If that's not a way to honor the past and get everyone connected to our core, I don't know what is. And clearly, doing this hasn't held us back.

The other thing is that our heritage and tradition may not be what many might immediately think of. Animation was the start of the organization, but it's one of many outcomes of who we are and what we do. While how we've done things has changed over the years, *what* we do never has—we tell stories. Storytelling is the very heart of our organization, and we can never forget that. Walt left a legacy of incredible storytelling and pushing the boundary of what's possible along the way. If we ever lost that and, say, pivoted to just selling pins, we would no longer be The Walt Disney Company.

Apple has achieved the success they have today because they know their organization fosters connection and have continued to evolve its technologies to do that, even after the unfortunate passing of Steve Jobs. An organization who didn't honor its heritage and traditions would likely not have succeeded after losing such a visionary leader. Whether by unforeseen external forces or the always-adapting nature of the free market, every organization continues to create new and better iterations of itself. If they can't remember what they originally looked like and respect those origins, the organization will eventually be unrecognizable—in a bad way.

To have gotten to where it has today, your organization must have been formed with some key foundational element that contributed to its success. That element is unique to your organization and executed better than most other organizations. This is how you had to have gained an initial foothold in the market to begin with. While your organization will have to innovate and progress to continue to succeed in an ever-changing world, that core element has to be upheld to maintain the defining x-factor of what the company does particularly well and must continue to do throughout its existence.

Your origins can either be the wind in your sails or the anchor holding you back, all depending on how you use it. Honoring your heritage and traditions is acknowledging the values and elements that your organization was founded with and carrying these things through each transformation of the business. Honoring your heritage and traditions is *not* dwelling in the past and allowing it to hamper innovation. It's all about embracing what you do, while being open to new takes on how you do it. That is the balance.

Key Takeaways

- **Your heritage is important, but it can be misused.** All good leaders have to find the balance between honoring the heritage without getting stuck in the past.

- **Honor where you came from.** Your organization's foundation has to have a unique element that led to its original success. This element has to be carried through each transformation of the business to retain the special x-factor and continue success on the market.

- **But don't get too comfortable.** If you get used to doing things a certain way because of precedents, you risk being unable to adapt when the market calls for it.

- **Let your foundation fuel you.** Ultimately, you need to be open to hearing new ideas on how you do things to further the ultimate purpose.

Integrity

Back when we talked about trust, there was a pretty brief mention on how a leader has to demonstrate a good character to build trust with their teams. Good character, high morals, strong principles, etcetera are all more or less just synonyms for "integrity." And integrity isn't just a necessity for building trust as a leader—it's an absolute necessity in leadership and life, period.

It's no secret that there is a small segment in leadership who are perhaps not in it for the right reasons, or even have the best intentions. Some people covet the title and shirk the actual responsibilities, while others wield their power only to benefit themselves. And some people might not be *bad*, really, but the way they act from one situation to another can be wildly different. A leader who does not always make decisions in the best interest of their teams and the purpose may not be a bad person, but they are definitely a bad leader. Why? Because they lack integrity.

When a leader lacks integrity, nobody can fully trust them and nobody can fully allow them to lead. It's a lot like democracy—you can't just come in and expect your team to follow you by strong-arming them into submission. A Civics 101 class will tell you that a legitimate government requires consent of the governed. To truly be an inspirational and effective leader, you have to get your teams to *let* you be their leader beyond simple designation. That takes trust, and a lot of it. And a big part of building trust is showing that you, as a leader, will act in a consistently upright and good way to the benefit of the organization. Which is...you guessed it... integrity.

Now, integrity is a very broad and multifaceted word. There are many things someone with integrity does, so it's impossible to pinpoint exactly one specific thing that makes someone have it. It's also not an episodic act, but a constant quality. You can't tell the truth once and decide you have integrity—you have to tell the truth, *always*. That truth might include a point of view that differs from others, but you have to tell it anyway. If you make one morally wrong choice or do something that's less than right even one time, you may not have much integrity after all. And if your teams see that, they'll start to lose trust and think less of you. That's just a natural consequence.

The easiest way to define integrity is simply by saying, "Do the right thing." And what does doing the right thing look like? Well, a lot of things. However, there are a few that just about everyone recognizes to be the right thing.

For one, doing the right thing is telling the truth. Honesty is one of the biggest tenets in most aspects of life. Having a foundation of integrity means you tell the truth at all times, to all people. If someone is doing something wrong, sit them down and walk them through the issue and how they can improve...immediately. If you are asked to give your opinion, give it. In fact, don't wait to be asked—if you have a strong opinion, share it. If something isn't working, say so. And if you screw up, own it. Tell it like it is, not like how you think others want it to be.

Being honest doesn't always win you favors. Being a Yes Dude and placating others at all times often does build rapport, but it doesn't last. A reputation and relationships built on this shaky foundation will eventually fall apart, while one built on honesty is enduring. You can be criticized on all other counts of your character, but when you consistently tell the truth, people will know and respect you for it. Sometimes, the truth hurts, but you have to tell it anyway. Honesty is the only way to grow as a person and help others improve along the way.

But I don't necessarily mean *brutal* honesty. It's your job to assess how the recipient will best take a message and communicate it to them in that way, and sometimes that takes a certain degree of sugarcoating. Mary Poppins sings that, "A spoonful of sugar helps the medicine go down," and you may have to do that from time to time. But there's a huge difference between tailoring the delivery of your message and changing the message itself. How you say it may differ, but *what* you are actually saying can never waver.

You always have to tell the truth, and you always have to make good on your promises. What good is your word if you don't keep it? When you go back on what you've said and fail to follow through, nobody will trust you to do anything. As a leader, this will tarnish your credibility and make people question your authority. In the practical sense, this does more damage than almost anything else.

Think about it like a parent with a child. Say the parent has taken them to the park and the kid keeps throwing sand. The parent says, "If you keep throwing sand, I'm taking you home." As kids do, they test the boundary and throw sand again. The parent says, "If you do that again, we're going home." They do it again, and the parent says, "I'm serious, do that one more time..." Do you think the kid is ever going to stop throwing sand? No. They know the threat isn't serious, so they will continue to do it because they continue to go unpunished. In an organization, your teams may start slacking off and doing whatever they want because they know you aren't *really* going to do anything about it.

On the flip side, say the parent tells that child they'll buy them a toy if they clean their room. The kid cleans their room, but the parent doesn't buy the toy. Too expensive, is their excuse. The parent says they'll go camping if the kid gets a shot without making a scene. The kid bravely sits through it, but the parent doesn't take them camping. They don't have time, is what they tell them. Now the parent promises they'll get ice cream if the kid does their homework. Do you think they'll actually do their homework? Probably not. They know the reward won't really be given, so they have no reason to do anything. If you do not deliver on any promised rewards to your teams, they will only feel disheartened when you attempt to incentivize them.

If you agreed to do something, show up and do it. If you shook on a deal, the deal is done. If you promised something, deliver it. And if for any reason you can't keep your word, communicate that honestly and upfront to the people you are going to let down. Constantly breaking promises is bad parenting and creates wayward teams, and does not bode with good integrity.

While integrity has to always be abided by and upheld 100% of the time, that's not actually realistic. I told you to always tell the truth, and I'll do so myself right now and say that we can't all do the right thing all of the time. We all have personal flaws and subconscious beliefs that we need to identify and work on. Simply put, none of us are perfect. That's called being a human. As humans, we *will* make mistakes along the way.

Errors are inevitable, but that doesn't mean you don't have integrity. What matters here is that you are willing to recognize what you did, admit fault, and learn from it. Integrity means you accept that you are fallible and use your mistakes as teaching moments to further your self-development. It takes vulnerability, humility, and a whole bunch of other things we've covered to do this, but that is what integrity in action looks like.

Sometimes, you may not see your mistakes and will need another pair of eyes to show you. When someone tells you that you've messed up, you need to at the very least hear them out and try to understand where they're coming from. Often, you'll find that a different perspective can point out where you might have an unconscious bias, a lack of knowledge, or some other blindspot that you'd never see otherwise.

While they may not always be right, someone who is willing to have this uncomfortable exchange with you—especially someone you know and trust—likely wouldn't put themselves out there like this if they didn't strongly feel like you were wrong, so you have to at least listen to what they're saying and genuinely take it into consideration. And when you are open to change after listening, you can further your development as a human and leader. I find that this contrarian thinking is one of the best enablers of broader thought.

In this way, getting called out can be really valuable for growth. Since others are willing to help you, then you should be willing to help others by calling them out when they are in the wrong. Sometimes it's just to stick up for someone else, and it probably won't help the offender. For example, if someone is belittling another person for their accent, they probably know that's wrong and choose to do it anyways. You can't unpack and correct deep-rooted bias in one exchange. But you can publicly draw that line in the sand and make it known that behavior is not right.

However, sometimes someone genuinely doesn't realize that what they've done or said is wrong, and they would greatly benefit from someone telling them so. As awkward as it may be, having integrity means you are willing to step up when the moment calls. It might not seem so in the moment, but this is really how you "pay it forward" and help others.

Integrity is a lot of things but, really, it's mostly about truth and constancy. If you act within your moral compass in every aspect of your life and value honesty even in difficult situations, you will demonstrate your integrity and gain your team's respect and approval along the way.

Key Takeaways

- **You need to demonstrate integrity in all aspects of your life, especially with your team.** They will not let you lead them if they don't think you are acting with integrity.

- **Integrity has many definitions, but it mostly means doing the right thing.** Doing the right thing includes telling the truth, sticking to your word, and growing from mistakes.

- **Honesty is always necessary.** While you may need to refine *how* you say something, the message itself always needs to be truthful.

- **Honoring your word is the only way others will respect it.** If you do not follow through on your promises, you will lose credibility with your teams and diminish your own authority.

- **Accept criticism and give it when needed.** Nobody is perfect. Being receptive to this kind of feedback and being willing to call someone out is how we can all see our mistakes and grow.

Balance Art and Science

The tricky thing about learning leadership in an academic sense is you will start to know just enough to be dangerous. By "dangerous," I don't mean this information will help you become an overlord and take over the galaxy or something. But sometimes when you have all of the tactics to lead and aren't yet comfortable in the actual *act* of leadership, you end up over-relying on what you know and become mechanical, not inspirational. This is why one of the most crucial aspects here is understanding how to balance the art and science of leadership.

The science is reading the data, understanding the tactics, and having expertise in your area of operations. That's an obvious prerequisite of leadership—you have to know how the machine works to run it. But it's the art of leadership, the crafted intuition you gain through experience, that makes the magic happen and ultimately creates inspiration. You develop an inner voice that grows stronger and stronger throughout the years as a leader, a great gift that you can't neglect. The art is how and when you decide to act on what you hear.

I've had many other leaders come to me for advice after they hit a decision-making crossroads. The data is telling them one thing, but their inner voice is telling them another—which one should they listen to? What I always say is, "Be a painter." You need to use the science to inform the art, sure, but your intuition will turn out to be correct way more often than the data ever does. There's a reason why all analytics come with a margin of error, after all.

Let's go further on that painting analogy. Say you're an artist sitting in a nice little studio overlooking the streets of Paris. You've got the best brushes in every size, premium paint in every color and shade, a perfectly-adjusted easel, a clean palette, and an untouched canvas. While these accessories are nice, does having them make you an artist? Are they going to jump up and do the work for you like the enchanted brooms in *Fantasia*? Of course not. Nothing is going to move until you decide to pick up a brush and put it to the canvas.

Everything you've learned and are given to guide your leadership—tactics, data, even this very book—are just tools for you to use as you see fit. You have to look down on the street and decide what scene you want to paint. Do you do a panorama of the entire block in your view, or a detailed closeup of just the calico cat walking along on the sidewalk to the left? Are you using bright, vivid colors, or more muted ones? Which brush to start? How much paint? How much pressure? Where? This is all up to you.

But here's the thing—in painting and in leadership, there is no one right way to go about it. Art critics rave about the photographically detailed paintings Vermeer did with debt-inducingly expensive materials as much as they do about the wild expressionist paintings that Basquiat did on the back of FedEx boxes. It's all about your tools and training—it's also about being brave enough to listen to your intuition and let it guide your hand, too.

At a theme park, especially one as large as Disney World, it is imperative that the many massive machines all run in harmony, so our industrial engineers play a major role in decision-making. Disney's industrial engineers are all very intelligent and educated people who have spent a lot of time out in the field doing measurements and collecting metrics. They know the numbers better than anyone else. Anytime they would give me these numbers, I'd always say, "Thank you for this data. Now, what do you recommend I do with this?"

I probably knew what I wanted to do with it about 90% of the time, but I really valued their perspective and wanted a fresh opinion. Sometimes it was difficult for them to feel comfortable enough to share their opinion, especially the younger engineers, and I'd have to push for it. "What are you?" I'd ask them. Their answer was always, "I'm an industrial engineer." I'd tell them that they have to rethink their title. Really, they weren't so much industrial engineers as *experience* engineers. They had the expertise to not only collect the data, but translate it into creating an incredible experience for guests. To really cement this reframing of their roles, I even formed an organization called Experience Engineering and Enablement to drive the point home. To be clear, I have a huge respect for industrial engineers...I just wanted to push their mindsets. Even those most within the science side of an organization are still very much artists, too.

Of course, science is *very* important. If all the data is telling you that replacing everyone's office chair with an exercise ball is a terrible idea and you heed your intuition instead, well, don't be surprised when the number of workplace falls rises. But the art can not be ignored. If everything you do and every choice you make is 100% by the book 100% of the time, you will marginalize your impact. Innovation only happens when people are willing to take a step back—with the data—and take the risk on their intuition.

Key Takeaways

- **The best leaders balance art and science.** They listen to the data and their intuition.

- **To be a painter means to use your tools.** You have to decide how to apply what you know and the information given within your leadership actions and choices.

- **Going strictly by the book never makes a real impact.** Art means taking risk, but data is not right 100% of the time either. You need to know when and how to follow your intuition.

- **Your inner voice is developed through years of experience.** It can be one of your most valuable tools to guide your leadership, and you have to learn to listen to it.

Presence

Throughout this book, I've given you quite a bit to think about. At this point, you probably have a lot of stuff bouncing around your head—you have to engage authentically and strategically develop your Circle of Influence, strengthen your core while also thinking holistically, honor your heritage as you continue transforming the business...and so on. As we've learned, these aren't paradoxes but rather fine lines that a leader learns to manage. There's so much you have to balance, consider, and attend to. Admittedly, this can get pretty overwhelming.

But it gets less complex over time. With enough experience, you'll find that you won't have to actively think about these things anymore. That's how you grow into your position as a leader—you eventually stop performing leadership tactics and start just, well, *leading*. This is really the goal.

I've previously said that leading means to "define your destination and go," but that's missing a few things. To say "define your destination and go, and be nimble and agile along the way," is better, but that doesn't quite cover it. What leading really means, in its complete and all-important essence, is this:

> Define your destination and go, and be nimble and agile along the way...and enjoy the journey there.

This is where presence, the magic word, comes in. I'd be remiss if I wrote a whole book on leadership and life without mentioning the most important thing about it. To do the best and get the most out of all aspects of your life, you need to be present while you're living it. And if you're constantly calculating for what *will* happen, you won't see what's actually happening around you. Be in the moment as it unfolds, or else you'll end up missing them entirely.

If we ever somehow got the chance to go back and re-experience our lives, every single one of us would choose to be more present and in the moment. But that's the thing—we can't go back. We only ever get one chance to experience our lives as they happen. One blink, and suddenly *right now* becomes a memory always growing more distant as we are propelled further on in time. We don't get to choose when it is most convenient for us to experience any one moment—if we don't use it, we lose it, and we lose it forever. It's now or never, all of the time.

Okay, that might've been a little heavy, but it is the truth. The sooner we can all accept the impermanence and fragility of life, the sooner we can all enjoy it to the fullest extent. When we understand just how precious and wonderful each moment is, we will appreciate every single one we get and try to always share that with others (because, yeah, relationships matter!). At the very least, we won't be so willing to waste the time we have on pointless conflicts, grudges, and other nonsense.

I think everyone gets my point, so I'll get off of my soapbox and switch over to what presence in leadership looks like. When we've talked about engagement, we've really only talked about engaging with the people around us. However, full and true engagement means engaging with the moment and place we're in, too. There's that saying, "Stop and smell the roses," and it's pretty apt here. Every once in a while, you need to pick your head up, look around, and appreciate everything going on.

That's not to say live completely and constantly in the moment. We can't all be wholly carefree, especially not leaders. You have to give some forethought for things and make your choices consciously and carefully to ensure you are doing the right thing. We have to learn the ropes, get the crew in order, determine the course, and figure out all the associated logistics before we can set off into the horizon.

But once you're out on the water and your sails are perfectly dialed in, it'd be such a waste not to take a minute to take it all in—the gentle rocking beneath your feet, the warm sun on your face, the salt in the air, anything and everything happening in the here and now. Remember, you won't get to do this later.

When you're in tune with the present, you'll also be attuned to any changes as they occur. The environment is always shifting, never stagnant—that's true anywhere. Blue skies and smooth waters could suddenly turn into a dark storm with little notice. Which captain do you think will be prepared—the one who goes out on the deck, or the one who stays locked in their quarters? You can never trust that the current conditions will stay the same. Things could be completely different from one moment to the next, and it's only by being in the moment that you'll be aware and able to pivot accordingly.

Regardless of your tenure as a leader, there's no question that, with your eyes and mind wide open, you can always learn some new things about leadership. You may or may not be a "new" leader, per say, but you are taking in new material and will need some time to fully synthesize it into your leadership. Right now, you are just getting yourself oriented on the boat. You're learning the names and functions of the pieces and parts that create the forward momentum, and it might take some time to remember them. You're starting to understand how to navigate, and what different situations call for. You're even taking your first turn at the wheel, but you're far from comfortable at it. With more experience, this will change.

There comes a point when you no longer have to run through a list of terms, protocols, and tactics to determine what you should do next. You won't have to consciously remind yourself of the difference between port and starboard anymore—they'll become navigational terms as simple and automatic as left and right. Every component of the boat will be as familiar to you as your own home is now, and you'll become completely comfortable at the metaphorical wheel of your ship. And when the winds start to change, you'll have developed the instinct to act without panic. Eventually, you'll just know what to do.

Being present isn't always easy, I get that. Presence is something I've had to learn over the years. Some people might be reading this and laughing at me talking about the importance of presence when I was known as a bit of a squirrel throughout my career. It has taken longer than I'd probably admit to be able to ignore the many distractions and focus on my here and now. So, trust me, I of all people understand that this can be challenging.

You might be scared to ease your grip on the wheel or take your eyes off of some future point. But you have to have enough trust in yourself and your team to step back and appreciate what you have now, because you may not have it later. In a world that's constantly striving for the future, you'll oddly find that being in the present will help you be a better leader by engaging authentically, adapting to changes more quickly…and enjoying each moment as it comes with the people around you.

Key Takeaways

- **We only get one chance to experience any moment.** If you do not choose to experience the moment as it unfolds, you'll miss it entirely.

- **You have to be present to authentically engage with the people around you.** When you aren't distracted by other things, you can connect with others right now.

- **Being in tune with what's currently happening means you'll be attuned to changes as they happen.** You'll be able to more quickly pick up on a change and make decisions to adapt to it.

- **Eventually, you won't have to actively think about leadership and simply *lead*.** Like piloting a sailboat, all these new concepts will eventually become second nature and you'll be able to set off without worry.

Feed the Good Wolf

Marty introduced me to this old Cherokee parable that goes something like this:

An elder is walking with his grandson when the young man asks him to share some of his life's wisdom. The old man thinks for a moment before telling him about the lifelong battle we all must face. In everyone, there is a good wolf and a bad wolf. The good wolf represents love, joy, peace, compassion, etcetera. The bad wolf represents greed, anger, arrogance, jealousy, etcetera. As the two are opposites, they are destined to forever fight for dominance within us. This is the conflict every single person experiences inside throughout their lives.

"Well, which one wins?" The boy asks.

"Easy," the elder replies, "the one you feed."

The story of the two wolves has led me to live a certain mantra: "Feed the good wolf." The same way that jedis must choose between the light and dark side, we all have to actively decide to give our energy and time toward the good wolf inside of us.

People have asked me before how I maintain positivity given all that life has brought to bear, including the loss of a son and having dealt with a long-term cancer diagnosis. Well, my outlook is that while life can definitely dish out some hard knocks sometimes, we all choose what we want to do with it. You ultimately get a return on your emotions—what you put out into the world is what you will receive. If you give into the impulses of the bad wolf—anger, jealousy, contempt, self-pity, and all the other negativity—that's all that will come back around. But if you rise above and choose to feed the good wolf—to be kind, compassionate, generous, and spread all things positive into the world—you'll soon receive that tenfold.

Each and every day, I choose positivity. That is my CHOICE and my choice alone, just like everyone else. I feed the good wolf. By feeding your good wolf, you will manifest and attract positivity. When you're focused on the good and don't needlessly dwell on the bad, life is just, well...better. And on the leadership side, when you're confident in yourself and others and maintain a realistic positivity, other people will take notice and will be more committed as a result. Whether we consciously know it or not, we want leaders who feed the good wolf, and that's ultimately who we all follow.

We can't ever get the two wolves to call a ceasefire and get along. That's just not their destiny. Our destinies, however, are self-determined. We can't control the wolves, but we can control which one gets fed. Where we spend our time, energy, and attention is ultimately what shapes our worlds. If we focus on the bad, then that's all we're going to see. If we try to focus on the good, we'll see that it far outweighs the bad and creates a better world...and build more commitment as a result.

It's mealtime for the wolves. You have a piece of meat in your hands. Throw it at the good wolf and let the bad wolf go hungry, or let the bad wolf feed and starve out the good wolf. It's up to you.

Key Takeaways

- **The good wolf and bad wolf is inside all of us.** They will fight forever, and we will always have to battle between positivity and negativity.

- **Our worldview and lives are shaped by which wolf we feed.** Where we focus our energy is what we'll get back in return.

- **By feeding the good wolf, we can create positivity in our lives and build commitment as a leader.** Your team will pick up on what you are manifesting and will ultimately follow a leader who feeds the good wolf.

- **While many things are out of control, you CHOOSE what you do with what life hands you.** You ultimately decide which wolf to feed.

Summary

- Leadership is the result of engagement and inspiration, but it's much easier said than done.
- By clearly communicating the destination upfront, your team will be able to get together and get there much faster, and pivot as needed along the way.
- While you get distanced from the day-to-day as a leader, you must continuously strengthen your core to ensure the organization continues to deliver its base.
- You have to gain Mastery and Command and Systems and Critical Thinking in order to lead holistically, which is a key responsibility in your position.
- Before you can transform your business, you first need to make sure it is running as well as it can in its current form.
- Because your organization's foundation is its defining x-factor that made it successful, you have to respect your heritage and tradition without getting stuck in the past.
- A leader has to have integrity, and having integrity means doing the right thing consistently and constantly.
- To be effective and inspirational, you have to choose how to use leadership concepts and tactics the way a painter would choose to use their art supplies.

- Define your destination and go—and enjoy the journey along the way, because you only get one chance to experience any moment.
- By feeding the good wolf, you can attract and manifest positivity that others will sense and follow you as a result.

CONCLUSION

If you've made it this far, thank you for riding this ride path and allowing me to share myself with you. I've told you about my life and career, the lessons learned and my musings on everything I've experienced so far. Hopefully, this has all provided you with some insight and teachings you can bring into your own life and leadership, and for me, it's been a focus every moment of every day. But if there is only one thing you take away from this book, it really is the three words I've said since the beginning—engage, inspire, lead. This is the heart and soul of everything we do as a human, neighbor, sibling, parent, spouse, friend, member of the community... and, of course, as a leader. Engagement creates inspiration and results in leadership. And why? Because relationships matter! It's as simple as that.

And like I said at the start, I never thought I'd actually sit down and write a book about this. I never thought I'd write a book, period. You might be wondering, *So why the change of heart, Jim?* Well, I had two compelling reasons that ultimately led to what you're reading now.

One, you already know I love engaging with others. I think I can offer a pretty cool perspective to the people around me. The trouble is, that's only so many people. I can dedicate the rest of my life to meeting new people and sharing what I know with them, and I would still only ever get to a fraction of a fraction (of a fraction) of everyone on this earth. I've come to realize that a book has the power to reach many more people than I ever personally could. If I can help even one person that I couldn't otherwise, then I have fulfilled my purpose here.

Two, I won't be able to engage with others on earth indefinitely. That's the fact of life after all—it's not forever, and I'm no exception to that. If there is one thing my journey with cancer has taught me, it's this. Marty has reminded me of the importance of leaving behind a legacy that lasts beyond the time I spend on this planet, something my friends and family can reflect on. In a way, this book is the legacy project that lets me continue engaging with others even when I'm looking down from above (hopefully!).

If you don't mind, allow me to indulge myself for a second and talk about the other physical piece of my legacy again, my window on Main Street. As I've said, one of the finest tributes one can receive upon the end of their career with Disney is a recognition of their contributions via a window on Main Street. I *never* really anticipated getting one. In fact, I assumed I wouldn't. I even prepared a soft response in case anyone asked about it when I retired. So it was a complete and incredible surprise when I came to find out that my name would look out over the thousands and thousands of guests who enter the Magic Kingdom each and every day. I mean, wow...that's really cool.

And while it is a wonderful honor, I would be remiss if I didn't call it for what it is—an episodic piece of glass. 99.99% of those who walk by and see it have no idea who I am. For what it literally is, the window is just a window.

It's what it represents that's important. I think of that window on Main Street as a symbol for the window into my heart. I keep this window open for you to always be able to look in and see how much I care about you, the people around me, and the relationships we all have with everyone. And, hopefully, you'll keep your window open for me. And, together, we can stay connected well beyond the bricks and mortar of the physical world.

At the end of the day, we can't take any of this with us. We exit this earth with nothing in hand. No cash, no cars, no windows. All we really have are the relationships we've built with others. So, in the time we do get, it wouldn't make sense not to use it connecting to and enjoying life with the people around us. Engage, inspire, lead. Nothing more to it.

SOURCES

Decade IV

Bennett, Nate and Stephen A. Miles. "Second in Command: The Misunderstood Role of the Chief Operating Officer." *Harvard Business Review*, May 2006, https://bit.ly/3y9buZe

Introduction to Inspirational Leadership

The Disney Institute team, et al. "Leadership Lessons From Walt Disney - How To Inspire Your Team." *Disney Institute*, 21 Mar. 2018, https://bit.ly/3zUYDeK

Engage: Relationships Matter!

"Engage, V. (5)." *Merriam-Webster*, https://bit.ly/3tRDRIU

Medhi, Barasha. "5 Fundamental Definitions of Employee Engagement." Business 2 Community, 17 Aug. 2020, https://bit.ly/3OamEm8

Humility and Vulnerability

Collins, Jim. *Good to Great: Why Some Companies Make the Leap and Others Don't*. HarperBusiness, 2001.

Brown, Brené. *Daring Greatly: How the Courage to Be Vulnerable Transforms the Way We Live, Love, Parent, and Lead*. Avery, 2015.

Trust

"Trust, *N.* (1)." *Merriam-Webster*, https://bit.ly/3xFxwS4

Matthews, Michael D. "The 3 C's of Trust." *Psychology Today*, 3 May 2016, https://bit.ly/3b5ZP4n

"Lady Gaga - Telephone ft. Beyoncé (Official Music Video)." *YouTube*, uploaded by Lady Gaga, 15 Mar. 2010, https://youtu.be/EVBsypHzF3U

Be Bold, Be Brave

"Teach girls bravery, not perfection | Reshma Saujani." *YouTube*, uploaded by TED, 28 Mar. 2016, https://youtu.be/fC9da6eqaqg

Inspire: Transform Hearts and Minds

"Inspire, *V.* (1)." *Merriam-Webster*, https://bit.ly/3QCAVK5

Make Work Fun

"Work, V. (1)." *Merriam-Webster*, https://bit.ly/3y9GSXz

Connect to Your Purpose

Sinek, Simon. "The Golden Circle Presentation." *Simon Sinek*, https://bit.ly/3n6SX9H

Sinek, Simon. *Start with Why: How Great Leaders Inspire Everyone to Take Action*. Portfolio, 2009.

Lead

"Lead, *V.* (1)." *Merriam-Webster*, https://bit.ly/3zRhirN

Introduction to Lead

Spider-Man. Directed by Sam Raimi, Columbia Pictures et al, 2002.

Lead with a Holistic Mindset

Wasserman, Tabitha. Article about an old English adage. *Medium*, 4 Feb. 2019, https://bit.ly/3zT5xRz

Heritage and Tradition

Plato. "Phaedrus." The Internet Classics Archive, https://bit.ly/3y9eYee

"Walt Disney Quotes." Disney Dreamer, https://bit.ly/3bnHqjW

ACKNOWLEDGEMENTS

Tom Staggs: Tom, I don't think you will ever realize the impact you had on me, and so many. You managed to bring to bear empathy, authenticity and drive. You will always be an iconic leader who leads with Influence, Credibility and a strong sense of collaboration. Thanks for always looking out for us and pushing us beyond our comfort zone without us even knowing it!

Meg Crofton: Meg, for so many years, you've been a beacon of authentic, driven, empathetic and strategic leadership. I've learned so much from you, especially as it relates to shaping thinking and moving cultures to places they didn't realize they could go to! I have always enjoyed our time together, and appreciate our friendship in "life after."

Catherine Powell: Catherine, you light up rooms, teams, and cultures. Thank you for always modeling excellence, and for making work fun. Your imprint is vast on our culture, and you always knew how to rally the troops...especially me! Your optimism, energy and drive was an amazing beacon of light for us all. Thank you for being who you are, and always respecting the views and voices of others.

Josh D'Amaro: Josh, I don't have the words to express how incredible you are, and how much I've ALWAYS enjoyed our time together. You make me smile at work or at play. Your conviction to make the world, especially ours, a better place is contagious. You kept us rolling during some incredibly challenging times. Josh, you are an incredible friend, and a model all of the essence of #LeadershipMatters!

Jeff Vahle: Jeff, your friendship, leadership and team focus is amazing. I've always enjoyed being around you and reflect fondly on all we accomplished together. We did some amazing things—thank you for making me think more deeply, reflect more methodically and for always being there for me, at work or at play. Thanks for always being you. #Oystersforever!

George Kalogridis: George, we've traveled together for a long time...literally and figuratively. Thanks for always maintaining a deep focus on what drives our business...our cast and our guests. Thanks for always looking out for me and caring, on both personal and professional fronts. I'll never forget our cross continent travels where we redesigned the world. Several times! I'll never forget that you traveled WAY out of your way to visit me at Mayo in Rochester, MN during my radiation. That meant the world to both Marty and me.

Al Weiss: Al, thank you for leading the Walt Disney World Resort through the most challenging times, and for your leadership presence at the global and local level. Your support of our NGE vision was a huge enabler to get through a lot of noise. Thank you for role modeling excellence.

Bruce Laval: Bruce, you are the smartest, most strategic leader I've worked for and been around. I learned so much from you on the nuts and bolts of our business. Thanks for being a great teacher for me and the team, and for teaching us how to think differently and never rest on our laurels. And for always pushing for excellence in all we endeavored to take on together.

Bob Lamb: OMG you know how to get a team jazzed to accomplish the impossible. You made work fun, and you cared deeply for those around you. You set the tone for me that said hard work can be fun. Thank you for all the years of successes and partnership, and thanks for sporting the Billy Bob teeth at the most opportune times with me.

Joe Schott: Joe, always loved our times together. Your business and operational savvy are unmatched...thanks for always being there to make things great. It's been so much fun to watch you grow with the company. I always said we ALL were going to work for you one day. Maybe I should have stayed longer to see that through! Thanks for your insights, wisdom, provocative thinking and your uncanny way to think holistically and end to end. And, congratulations on taking over the Face Man role. You've got this!

Tilak Mandadi: From the moment you landed on the WDW site, I knew that you were going to....save us!! Thank you for making immediate and dramatic improvements, and for being a great friend. In life, it's not about what we do, but how we've impacted others. Your impact on me is deep. From our shared experiences personally and professionally, it's an honor to call you my friend...hope the same your way! Keep being you, living life to its fullest and reminding those around you what's really important.

Ken Potrock: Ken, thanks for being a great friend and partner. You helped me understand early in my career the importance of thinking differently and pushing the envelope. Thank you for the years of collaboration...we did some pretty spectacular things together.

Kevin Lansberry: Kevin, thanks for your support throughout our time together. I've always enjoyed watching you in action, and often talk about the path you took across Ops, Alliances and Finance. Your deliberate effort to expand your knowledge base was impressive, and paid off in making you the leader you are today. Thanks for your support along the way.

Zach Riddley: Zach, thanks for being such a great friend, and a spectacular creative leader. We had a lot of fun together over the years, and I've always appreciated your candid perspective. Congrats on all you've done, and the impressions you've made on many. Very grateful.

Erin Wallace: Erin, thank you for your friendship and support throughout the years. You were one of the very first individuals to lay eyes on the kiddos in NICU...I'll never forget how supportive you were to both Marty and I throughout the years. We had so much fun at DAK opening...and we killed it. Thanks for sending a lifeline in my return back to Orlando in 2002. I will be forever grateful for our friendship and for all we accomplished together.

Claire Bilby: Claire, I can't begin to thank you enough for your friendship and partnership. Way back in the Disney-MGM Studios when we were starting the events business, you taught us how to do it right. Since then, between east coast, west coast etc you've always been a bundle of energy and someone whose passion and integrity I so admire. Thank you for being such a great friend over the years. Please invite me to your New Year's Day parties forever.

Melissa Valiquette: Melissa, watching you grow has been one of the most exciting and enjoyable parts of my career. You lead with an incredibly strong presence, and your courage, coupled with your drive, is awesome to watch in action. I've enjoyed learning from you in all aspects of life, at work AND at play. And you are one heck of a salsa dancer! I'm so hopeful that we can continue to stay connected. Keep being you!! Abrigato!!

Roz Durant: From the minute we met I knew we were destined for extraordinary friendship and an incredibly dynamic leadership team. Thanks for always shooting straight, for your strong faith and for your courage and commitment to what we do. You made work fun and challenged thinking in a healthy and inspiring way. I know we will be connected in "life after" work and all else.

Maribeth Bisienere: OMG how we have traveled steep mountains, impossible terrain and marched toward accomplishing the impossible. Your friendship and our connections even beyond work have been invaluable. You are a role model as a business leader, community leader, great mom and spouse, and you lead with such strong faith. Grateful for our time together and for your role modeling strong focus on faith and family.

Thomas Mazloum: Thomas!! How fun it was to spend time with you. You have an uncanny way of peeling back your business and rebuilding it to a better place. You have such incredible multi industry experience that was so valuable to all of us the moment you arrived. Thanks for always looking out for me AND making sure I didn't "GO TESLA" too much, especially since I don't own one. I so appreciate it and you. Continue modeling for others your innate ability to constantly and relentlessly Feed the Good Wolf.

Nate Wilson: Nate...it's been fun watching you grow as a husband, dad, leader and friend. Proud of all you accomplished and contributed to our success, for your honesty and transparency, and for your support of some of the wacky things we took on. Appreciate you. And in the words of Mufasa, remember who you are. Fix your business card!

Scott Hudgins: Hey...we've traveled some miles and rough terrain together! Thanks for always being thoughtful and strategic and pushing those around you to think next level. I've always appreciated our friendship and partnership.

Jason Kirk: Do you remember being EAGLE 1 during our DLR days? You were a young, upcoming IE when we first met, and it was obvious that you had a brilliant future ahead of you. Yes, you certainly had BIG SHOES after I left, LOL, and I am so proud of all you've done literally around the world, and especially domestically. You are a role model husband, father, and leader. Keep going and remember to light people up!!

Phil Holmes: Phil...our miles traveled together are many. I've always appreciated your friendship at work or at play, your operational savvy, and your ability to continue to think provocatively and innovatively. You were always willing to step out there with me, and I'm very grateful for that. Thanks for always being there for me and with me, and for the legacy you left for all. Nice sharing a window pane with you!

Deb Hart: Where do I begin...you are an amazing human being on all dimensions. There's not an effort I would ever take on without having you playing a major role in it. Your ability to shape thinking, influence the broader org and deal with ambiguity is uncanny. I appreciate you so much as a leader, friend, mom, spouse etc. Your faith in God fueled me so many times and you uplifted me often during my most challenging health journey(s). Thank you for being you.

Sarah Riles: OMG how I think about the time we've been together and the amazing things we've done. I've always loved your curiosity, courage and tenacity, on balance with recognizing the soft skills of leadership. I'm very proud of you for all you've accomplished and grateful to have had you in my life.

Djuan Rivers: Djuan, although we didn't have a lot of years working directly together, I've always admired you for your energy and enthusiasm, creativity and fun. It was a blast working with you these latter years, your zest for life and your living your best self is an example for all. And...I enjoy sharing our pane (window) together!!

Jon Storbeck: Jon, I'll never forget our time together at DLR. From the moment we met, you were clearly a man / leader of integrity. A rare trait in those days, lol! Thanks for always being you. For being a role model husband, father and leader. I love seeing you living your best life right now...all things for a reason and the world at large is better with the impact you have on it personally and professionally. I'll always remember your best teaching: "Do The Right Thing." You have, and I know you always will.

Neil Simmons: Neil, it has been such a treat to be able to call you a friend, first and foremost, and someone who always answers the last minute, emergency phone call with such optimism and "get it done" energy. My favorite time together, of course, was our hiking the Appalachian Trail. OMG was that fun. And we learned a different commodity of trade...you want some of my trail mix? LOL. Thanks for always being there for me. I respect and appreciate you so much!

Dennis Higbie: Dennis, you've always been such an optimistic force of energy and creativity. You model excellence in both understanding your craft, and bringing generalist leadership alive. My fondest memory is when you shared with me that you planted a tree on the top of Kali River Rapids in my mom's name, who passed during the opening of DAK. I still don't have the words to express my gratitude. Thanks for being a great friend, and an extraordinary leader!!

Ketan Sardeshmukh: DUDE...you rock. Thanks for always bringing your best self forward, for sitting in "the hot seat" and driving the business, and for being a master integrator of our business. You are an incredible friend, dad, spouse and being. #Appreciate you.

Shari Schmitt Wiggins: Shari...H1—my oh my, the stories we could tell. We've traveled together through tragedy and joy, and I am ever so grateful our paths crossed when they did. I so appreciate your selfless giving to others, your masterclass efforts RIKCing, and the positive attitude you've always had on life. I've loved watching you raise the girls and finally focus on yourself. Proud of you for who you are and how you live life.

Natalie Sirianni: Nat, I don't even know where to begin. H3, we've traveled a lot of miles together, on flat roads and steep mountains. I knew the minute we met that you would be a critical partner for me in the endeavors to come. Your sense of logic, ability to read between the lines and understand the direction we were going to travel well before I got the map out is amazing. One of us would think it...the other would say it. Scary! You are an extraordinary business partner, spouse, mom and a great friend of so many. I know we will stay connected throughout our time on this planet and beyond. We would not have accomplished the impossible without your presence. Thanks for ALWAYS being you and bringing your best in everything you do in life.

Kristen Barthel: Kristen...I've got a smile a mile wide as I write this. OMG could we write our own book. I've always appreciated you for who you are, for the values you live by and for always working so hard to seek the truth in the fog.

You are a confidant, a truthteller and a driver of excellence. Your future is so bright, at work and at play. Thanks for being such a valued friend and partner. You role model excellence in all aspects of your life. I am better having met you, and wish we had more time together!

Sheri Torres: Sheri…thank goodness we got those cobwebs cleaned up together! I appreciate you so much…you were always there for the organization and for me. You helped me think through challenging times, and great times. You are a partner of choice and I am grateful for the years we had together. I've loved every minute of our time together. Watching you at work and in your personal life be a leader is impressive. Thanks for all you've taught me and helped me with—Forever Grateful!

Wende Bendik: Oh my. Wende. H2, the fun we had at Epcot, and beyond. Thanks for going for the ride with me. I always appreciated your perspective, and more important, who you are and how you lead.

Judy Terry: Over? Never Over. YOU are amazing and your positivity is contagious. Thanks for always looking out for me, taking care of me and all around you. You light up the room with your willingness to jump in. I'm forever grateful to have had the chance to work so closely together.

Jennifer Dutton: Although our time together was short, I'm grateful for having had the chance to work with you and spend time together. You helped lead us through some very challenging times, and I'll always be thankful for that.

Debbie Snow: Deb, thanks for being such a great partner and friend during our time together. You are the consummate networker and can get the impossible done in the blink of an eye. You know how to bring fun to a fast paced environment, and you and I made one hell of a Homecoming King and Queen for DAK pre-opening!

Reesa Martin: Hey! Reesa, you have the most incredible heart and give so much to those around you. Thanks for always thinking of me during the fun times and the more challenging one. I've appreciated our friendship and your support throughout many decades. I'm very grateful for all you've done for me.

Nancy Belanger: My oh my...we've known each other for SO LONG but only had a chance to spend our last couple years together...I'm grateful for you, your network, your values and your innate desire to collaborate so well. You have a knack for extracting the truth out of folks...very cool. Thanks for making these last couple of years bearable!

Kelly Novitski: Kelly, it's been such a joy watching you come into the organization and make an immediate, tangible impact. You have the classic albeit rare DNA of an incredible integrator in so many ways. We did a lot of fun, crazy things together—honored to call you my friend.

Carrie Sandusky: Carrie...can't thank you enough for all you've done for me, the team and the broader organization. Watching you grow into who you are has been amazing and rewarding. Thanks for always "doing the right thing" and for always having the ability to get us back on track. Appreciate you.

Teri Rosenfeld: Teri, one would have to look far and wide to find an executive, and human being, with the vast and diverse experience that you bring each and every day. And oh my goodness, could we tell some stories. I've always admired you for your forward thinking, optimism and energy. Way back when, whether in the LOB, or to/from Tallahassee with oysters (bad ones) enroute, we always had a blast together. You've forgotten more than most will learn over a lifetime on how wonderful, and challenging, running an operation is. It was fun to do that together. Thank you for many great memories, and for being you.

Meg Patten, Sarah-Jane Josef and Jaclen Lapham: Hi "A" team...thanks for generating great content and always "Riding the Ride Path" for me. You all brought great stories to life in such incredible ways. I always knew you had my back while we were changing the world!! You All Rock!!

Scot Reynolds: Dude... we've traveled across this landscape on many different paths, doing many extraordinary things. I've always appreciated your integrity, your values, your ability to connect the dots, and then get everyone going. You are a great friend...thanks for always bringing your A game forward. As Doc Holliday said to Wyatt…"I'll always be your huckleberry"!

Joe Kalla: Surfs' up. Thanks for being a great friend and a great leader, and for never compromising your values and beliefs. I've appreciated our friendship for some time, and even more, your contributions to the team. Our times surfing Cabo, east coast AND TYPHOON LAGOON were such a blast. Keep being you!

Val Bunting: Val, you will forever be one of the most optimistic, energetic leaders and friend that I've ever had the pleasure to be around. You were always willing to take on the challenges that seem to come at us like a Tsunami, and I'm forever grateful to have crossed paths and have as much fun as we did!

Trevor Larsen: Trevor, it's been a great run leading / hanging out with you. We took on a lot together, and I have always been grateful that you'd answer my calls, because it was usually due to a crisis that only you could get us out of. Thanks for role modeling life…I enjoy sharing our window together.

Beth Stevens: Dr, Dr…..my oh my do we have a lot we could share. Thanks for coming into Disney and shaping the future of Animal Care, Conservation and the Environment. I learned so much from you, and we made a heck of a team. Thanks for always thinking about our family, and for caring so much. The world is literally a better place because of your passion, energy and drive.

Greg Emmer: Greg, thanks for the great times…transportation, MK ops, MK entertainment, Park Ops line of business, etc. You pushed hard but with empathy and defined the essence of Operational Excellence. Thanks for taking this neophyte on hiking expeditions, Appalachian Trail, west coast mountain ridges, etc. You and Jan are incredible role models for so many aspects of life. I've always appreciated our friendship.

Lee Cockerell: Lee, thanks for your leadership over the years and for supporting my move back from Cali during 9/11, such a difficult time in the world! Forever grateful!

Rena Langley: Hey!! I had a wonderful time getting to know you during our somewhat brief time together. You have endless stamina and as I've always said the hardest job ever. You do it with grace and dignity. Thanks for allowing me to get to know you and for the times we had together.

Dan Soto: Dan, I've always been in awe of how you lead your life…at work and at play. Your drive and stamina is amazing, and you were the glue for NGE…and look at you now!! Thanks for always being you!

Gary Daniels: Care Bears and Rainbows! #Never Forget. You are a strong leader, strong man of faith and a wonderful husband and dad. I'm so glad we got to know one another, and know you will always be amazing in all you do.

Mark Kirchof: From driving boats and monorails 45 years ago, to sitting in your pickup at the 711, to hitting the chain of lakes, to watching you as an incredible husband, dad, grandpa, Air

Force aviator and commercial pilot has been awe inspiring. You and Bev are incredible parents...Steve, Katie and Kari have grown into their own and are so amazing. Most important—thank you for you so much more...you've always been there for me in good times and dark times. Always on the ready to lend a hand. I'm honored to call you my best bud, and even more looking forward to jumping into next chapters for both of us.

Burke Grant and Doug Bryant: Together we were the three musketeers. Thank goodness social media didn't exist back then. We lived life large and I am so grateful we still stay connected. Proud of you both and the friendship, laughter and fun we continue to have. And that we are still alive. KENS MUG #328 ALWAYS ON THE READY.

Renaut van der Reit: Renaut, you changed my life and that of my family. Your commitment to God, your ability to transform hearts and minds and your role as a family leader and community leader is so important and you do it so well. Thanks for joining me on the surf session in Costa Rica and for discipling me toward the true path of faith.

Zoe Rose: Zoe, thank you for being my partner in crime on this endeavor. I've so enjoyed getting to know you, listening to your thoughts and feedback and watching you grow. Your partnership on this effort significantly "occupied" my first year of retirement! They say that's a hard adjustment but working with you allowed me the freedom to reflect on my life and career with renewed energy. You are extraordinarily talented, and your future is incredibly bright. I look forward to watching you take over the world! #FriendsForever!

Dan, Kathy, Scott MacPhee and my nieces and nephews: I guess when you "get to be my age," you start to think about and remember the incredible family times more and more. We were blessed with incredible parents who showed us how to live a great life and fulfill our DREAMS. I am so proud of you in who've you become and the role model you serve as great parents. So many great memories from our early years. We all found our different paths and hobbies, but remained connected throughout the journey. I am forever grateful for that, and for you. To Andrew, Sarah, Michael, Addison, Laurel, Michael and Colin...as Papa Mac used to teach us, keep on dreaming and always remember to Live, Laugh, Love, Listen and Learn! I'm still trying!

Carter MacPhee: Carter, my pride and love for you goes to infinity, and beyond. Watching you grow up and live your life has been amazing. Your creativity, curiosity, depth of knowledge on all the things that make you curious is so impressive! You have a strong desire for mastery in everything you do, and your future is so incredibly bright. Thank you for teaching me about so many things in life...how to be a better husband, dad, leader and friend. I am so proud of you for your bravery in your authentic self and advocating for so many. I am so proud to be your dad. I love you to the moon and back, and back again!!

Anna MacPhee: Anna, just writing your name puts a big fat smile on my face. It's been an incredible honor to watch you travel through life. Your energy, optimism, bravery and creativity is palpable. You light up the world—it's so fun to watch you enter the room and light it up. You have a sharp and witty sense of humor...never lose that and keep it going!! The future is incredibly bright for you...your conviction for relationships and strong business savvy is going to serve you well. Watch Out World! Thanks for teaching me so much, as well. I am so proud to be your dad. I love you endlessly.

∧JJ MacPhee∧: Our Son, your time on this planet was short, but your impact on the world remains profound. Thank you for keeping an eye on us from above and ensuring that we live our best lives. Thanks for being a fantastic wingman for Anna, Carter, mom and me, and for getting camp set up for our arrival one day, and for keeping an eye on Papa Mac and Mom, and all those we love and cherish above. We love you and miss you.

Cabo MacPhee: Cabo, you are a bundle of energy and unpredictability. Thanks for keeping us protected wherever we go, and for always making us smile with your four legged prance. I love our walks together, and love watching mom love on you, and vice versa. You are a good boy!!

Papa and J Sevenich: J and Papa, thank you from the bottom of my heart for bringing Marty into this world and for always being there for us. Thanks for putting up with all of us, especially me. You have shaped me and the entire family in so many ways. So grateful for all you've done for us!

Marty MacPhee: Baby, there are no words that can be written in a book that could describe my deep love and gratitude for you. When GOD appointed angels to their assignments, you may have drawn the short straw, but there is no question he was looking out for me. Thanks for keeping me alive, literally and figuratively. As my wife, friend, confidant, teacher and role model, you show me and so many others the way in your actions and deeds. You always do the right thing. I stand in awe watching you live your life as a spouse, mom, industry leader, consultant and great friend of many. Your curiosity, courage and bravery is so amazing. I love you truly, madly, deeply.

ABOUT THE AUTHOR

Jim MacPhee began his career with Walt Disney World in the summer of 1978 and retired as Chief Operating Officer / Senior Vice President, Operations on April 1st, 2021.

In a career spanning over 42 years, Jim has functioned in a variety of roles across all of the theme parks at both *Walt Disney World*® in Orlando, Florida and the *Disneyland*® Resort in Anaheim, California.

He began his career in the summer of 1978 as an hourly cast member driving the Watercraft vessels in Bay Lake and the Seven Seas Lagoon just outside the Magic Kingdom. He performed a variety of different roles at various levels across all of the theme parks, and was promoted in 1996 to the executive position of General Manager of Disney's Animal Kingdom. In this role, Jim was responsible for the operational input, development, and opening of the park. Shortly thereafter, in 1999, Jim went to California to be a part of the opening team for Disney's California Adventure at the Disneyland Resort as Vice President, Attractions & Guest Services.

In the spring of 2002, Jim returned to Walt Disney World, and in 2004 was promoted to Vice President of Park Operations Development, Optimization, and Standardization, where he led a team focused on the development and delivery of Operational Excellence across the properties. In early 2007, Jim accepted the role of Vice President, *Epcot*®, a position he held until March 2009, when he was assigned to lead the transformation of the Walt Disney World vacation experience via the introduction of *MyMagic+*, resulting in co-authorship of multiple patents in the creation and introduction of experience technology enhancements.

In 2010, he was promoted to the role of Senior Vice President, Walt Disney World Parks and was responsible for the strategic direction of all four theme parks at Walt Disney World, in addition to operationalizing My Magic + across the site's landscape. He led the Vice Presidents of Magic Kingdom, Epcot, Disney's Hollywood Studios, and Disney's Animal Kingdom, who oversaw daily operations and more than 30,000 Cast Members. During his eight years in this role, Jim advanced Walt Disney World Parks through a long-term strategic plan, focused on unprecedented enhancements of the Guest experience and expansion efforts across the resort, significantly improving cast, guest, and business results along the way.

In January 2018, Jim was promoted to the role of Chief Operating Officer/Senior Vice President, Walt Disney World Resort. This role covered all site operations, including four theme parks, over 20 resorts, premium experiences, college housing, transportation, Disney Springs, security, two water parks, and the ESPN Wide World of Sports Complex. His team also oversaw the long-term strategic planning and day-to-day operations of Disney Live Entertainment, Food and Beverage, Experience Optimization and Planning, and the Guest and Cast Experience. In total, his leadership spanned more than 50,000 Cast Members across the Walt Disney World Resort.

In the spring of 2020, Jim played the lead role for the Walt Disney World site in managing the pandemic-driven strategic and executional phases of closure, downtime, and re-opening, which included preparing and presenting the re-opening plans to local and state government officials. The Walt Disney World site reopened mid-July and has successfully operated in this new environment, with consistently favorable site inspections by government officials and high consumer confidence measures in the delivery of all safety related protocols.

Born in Illinois, Jim considers himself an "almost native Floridian," having been raised in Ormond Beach and attended Florida State University. Jim is an active member of the Executive Board of Florida Hospital.

Dedicated to his family, Jim and his wife Marty have two children, Anna and Carter. As a family, they enjoy spending time together on the Florida coastlines and trails.

Made in the USA
Monee, IL
01 August 2022